THE EVENING WAS SIMPL...

Police in Bangkok arrested a gang of ... tourists complained that the gang first lured them to suck their nipples, then robbed them. The nipples had been covered with tranquilizers to put the victims to sleep.

WHERE'S THE BETTER BUSINESS BUREAU

when you need it? At least six people who paid $2.50 each to visit a Memphis zoo exhibit called "Dinosaurs Live!" demanded their money back after discovering that the creatures weren't real, but only computerized, mechanical replicas.

AND FOR ONLY 11% INTEREST, HE'LL MOO

When the loan department at a San Antonio, Texas, Bank One branch informed a 40-year-old customer that his loan application had been denied, he took off all his clothes, sat down in the office of the vice president for loans, and began to quack. When police arrived, he continued to quack in response to their questions.

RALPH KRAMDEN, CALL YOUR OFFICE

Ann Smith, 38, of Rotherham, England, left her husband after nine months of marriage due to what she felt was his unusual obsession with buses. Mark Smith, 29, took his new bride on a tour of bus garages on their honeymoon, became angry when she neglected to clean his collection of 36,000 bus photos, and crashed Ann's car while he was looking at a bus, sending her to the hospital with head injuries.

JOHN J. KOHUT, a political analyst, has been collecting strange news clippings for more than a decade. **ROLAND SWEET** is a magazine editor and the author of his own syndicated column. Together they collected *Countdown to the Millennium* and, along with Chuck Shepherd, compiled *News of the Weird, More News of the Weird,* and *Beyond News of the Weird* (all Plume). Both live in the Washington, D.C., metro area.

JOHN J. KOHUT & ROLAND SWEET

NEWS FROM THE FRINGE

True Stories of Weird People and Weirder Times

Illustrations by Drew Friedman

A PLUME BOOK

PLUME

Published by the Penguin Group
Penguin Books USA Inc., 375 Hudson Street,
New York, New York 10014, U.S.A.
Penguin Books Ltd, 27 Wrights Lane, London W8 5TZ, England
Penguin Books Australia Ltd, Ringwood, Victoria, Australia
Penguin Books Canada Ltd, 10 Alcorn Avenue, Toronto, Ontario,
Canada M4V 3B2
Penguin Books (N.Z.) Ltd, 182–190 Wairau Road, Auckland 10, New Zealand

Penguin Books Ltd, Registered Offices:
Harmondsworth, Middlesex, England

First published by Plume, an imprint of Dutton Signet,
a division of Penguin Books USA Inc.
Copyright © John Kohut and Roland Sweet, 1993
Illustrations copyright © Drew Friedman, 1993

First Printing, November, 1993
1 3 5 7 9 10 8 6 4 2

 REGISTERED TRADEMARK—MARCA REGISTRADA

LIBRARY OF CONGRESS CATALOGING IN PUBLICATION DATA
Kohut, John J.
News from the fringe : true stories of wierd people and wierder
times / John J. Kohut & Roland Sweet ;
illustrations by Drew Friedman.
p. cm.
ISBN 0-452-27095-2
1. Curiosities and wonders. I. Sweet, Roland. II. Title.
AG243.K62 1993
031.02—dc20 93–24734
CIP

Printed in the United States of America
Set in Century Expanded and Tekton Bold Oblique

Designed by Steven N. Stathakis

BOOKS ARE AVAILABLE AT QUANTITY DISCOUNTS WHEN USED TO PROMOTE
PRODUCTS OR SERVICES. FOR INFORMATION PLEASE WRITE TO PREMIUM
MARKETING DIVISION, PENGUIN BOOKS USA INC., 375 HUDSON STREET, NEW
YORK, NEW YORK 10014.

To Lissa and Theo

Acknowledgments

We are indebted to the keepers of court records and police blotters, to official spokespersons—to officialdom in general—and to tireless reporters and copy editors whose papers tell the strangest stories in just two inches. We are especially grateful to the periodicals cited at the end of this volume.

John thanks family, friends and longtime contributors Jim, Jamie, Bill, Susan, Jonathan, Charlie, Dick, Greg, Heidi, Joe, Janet, Roxanne, Libby, Peter, Bonnie, Bandit, Pansy, Tillie, and Jake.

Roland thanks minutiae militia members Jim Turosak, Roger LeDuc, D. Kingsley Hahn, Kihm Winship, Mike Greenstein, and Rick "L. Richard" Mariani.

We're grateful to Gail Ross for her support and encouragement, to Howard Yoon for telling us where to be and when, and to Jennifer Romanello for helping us spread the weird.

Thanks to Ed Stackler for bringing this book to life and to Drew Friedman for his own vision of weirdness.

Special thanks to all the aficionados of weirdness who've sent us clippings over the years and to Dick Wien, who brought truly weird news, with actual photographs, to supermarket checkouts everywhere.

As usual, we owe it all to Chuck Shepherd, for his inspiration and example. And for permitting us access to The Chuck Shepherd Castoff Archives.

Finally, in the beginning, there was Charles Hoy Fort, who lived to clip.

Contents

Introduction

The times, they are a-stranging. Our unabating accumulation of puzzling evidence proves it. Our previous chronicle, *Countdown to the Millennium*, documented nearly 600 cases, each one certified true by the newspapers that reported them. Barely a year later, we've gathered 600 more.

These dispatches from the fringe pretty well cinch it that people are caught up in a frenzy of folly. We're not entirely unconvinced that this strange behavior is the manifestation of humanity's subconscious recognition of the approaching year 2000 as the foretold Millennium. A splinter group is trying to buy some time by pointing out that, technically, the new millennium doesn't start until 2001, but what's a year when you're talking the End of the World? Judging from what we read in the newspapers, people are behaving like these really are the last days of the planet.

Sure, the news sounds ominous. That doesn't mean it's all serious, or the laughter all nervous.

It is this occasional hilarity that the title *Countdown to the Millennium* failed to convey adequately about the book's actual contents. If you passed it up for that reason and, now that you know it isn't a Bible-thumping tract about Armageddon, wish you had bought it, don't panic. Copies remain. Our three earlier collections, *News of the Weird*, *More News of the Weird*, and *Beyond News of the Weird* (compiled with Chuck Shepherd), also are prodigiously in print. All four titles are in the *humor* section.

The title of this book might as easily be *News for the Fridge*. America's refrigerator doors hold many of these journalistic curiosities, which are a subcategory of the news best described as:

Dog bites man: no news.

Man bites dog: news.

Man bites man: news from the fringe.

Here's just a hint of what we're talking about:

Monkey vandals, Haile Selassie found (bet you didn't know he was missing), Giant Tusked Wetas, roadkill art, dagger guns, fire ants attack, cow dung high, armed animals, ominous clowns, exploding TVs, serial statue bomber, "Yahoo!," dumpster diving video, Silent Meeting Club, "Towns That Hum," killer pandas on the loose, three words—Oil Tank Party!—Mao's back, 20,000 noses, monkey trade union, Illinois mystery circles, Gulf Breeze Six return, drawbridge diving, mystery wave, sleep-related eating disorders, carrot addicts, weird sex, people who can't leave the dead alone, Rent-A-Family, 666 news, used dildos, Columbus curse (knock on wood), Anti-Nap Man, sex maniac trading cards, prairie dog vacuum, shotgun funerals, goo-oozing hairy potatoes, stinking bills, mystery critters, White House karate attack, giant fungus on the move, no swallows return to Capistrano, Virgin Mary sightings, self-surgery, Bushu-suru, nose-picking study (funding no problem) . . .

Strange days indeed. Strangely real. Frighteningly hilarious. And this is just part of what we've been able to uncover, two guys without even a government grant reading as many newspapers as we can. (Mick Jagger once asked the question, "Who wants yesterday's papers?" Now you know, we do.) After 20 years spent elbow deep in newsprint, we continue to be dumbfounded by what we read. You, we guarantee, will be utterly amazed!

If you're already on to the same strangeness we're seeing and your own refrigerator door is thick with yellowed clippings, please share them with us at this address:

> *Strange News*
> *P.O. Box 25682*
> *Washington, D.C. 20007*

Now, here's the developing situation on Earth. . . .

1

Strangers in a Strange Land

IT'S ONLY A MOVIE!

AT LEAST SIX PEOPLE WHO PAID $2.50 each to visit a Memphis zoo exhibit called "Dinosaurs Live!" demanded their money back after discovering that the creatures weren't real, but only computerized, mechanical replicas. "We thought when we opened we would have kids who would be frightened by the dinosaurs," said Ann Ball, a zoo vice president. "But little did I know I would have adults who didn't know dinosaurs were dead."

SOLOMON AND MONA FROMMELL, BOTH 37, fought their eviction from the Parker Apartments in DeSoto County, Florida, by claiming to have established their own country and announcing that their apartment was now their embassy. Proclaiming themselves the new president and ambassador of the "Adherent Paradise Government of the United States," the Frommells painted a line around their parking space, explaining that it was the embassy boundary. They insisted that they did not recognize the government of the United States.

Neighbors said that the couple often barricaded their door, leaving and entering their "embassy" through the windows. On the day their second eviction notice was served, they attacked sheriff's deputies with a butcher knife and a nunchaku. When a SWAT team was summoned to remove them, the Frommells declared the action amounted to a "kidnapping."

THE 1992 ANNUAL ST. LOUIS RIVERFRONT easter egg hunt was canceled because of the way parents behaved at the 1991 hunt. They broke through a yellow police ribbon, rushed past children, knocking many of them over, and pushed aside Boy Scout volunteers, all in a grab for the 20,000 hidden eggs. Thomas W. Purcell, chairman of the organizing committee, explained that the parents had been a problem for the three previous hunts, each year exhibiting more aggressive behavior.

Another hunt had to be canceled in South Portland, Maine, because parents that same year trampled over children to beat them and each other to the prizes. According to Debi Smith of the Parks Department, they "scarfed up everything like vacuum cleaners."

THE STATE UNIVERSITY OF NEW YORK'S Maritime College hired Joseph Hazelwood, former captain of the ill-fated *Exxon Valdez*, to be the watch officer for its cadets training cruise from New York to Gibraltar. A jury found Hazelwood guilty of negligence in the 1989 accident when his tanker struck a reef and dumped 11 million gallons of crude oil in the worst oil spill in U.S. history. He lost his license for nine months after pleading no contest to drinking within four hours of sailing and leaving a third mate in charge of the bridge.

POLICE CHARGED SERGIO HERNANDEZ,

28, with looting during the 1992 Los Angeles riots after finding stolen television sets stored in his home. Hernandez was a 1989 state lottery winner who receives $120,000 a year in winnings.

POLICE IN CEDAR RAPIDS, IOWA, FOUND 15

trees in a city park fitted overnight with doorknobs and locks set about three feet off the ground. The doorknobs were placed on opposite sides of each tree as if to suggest that a person could open one side, pass through and close the other side. In an apparently unrelated story, a few days later in New York City, more than 100 doorknobs were reported missing from public lavatories.

THE HEALTH MINISTER OF COLOMBIA

closed the dissecting room of the medical school of the Free University in Barranquilla after police discovered that a gang of university security guards had lured more than 30 people there and then shot or clubbed them to death and sold their bodies to the medical school for $200 each.

IN JUNE 1992, A SERIAL STATUE BOMBER

struck Stockholm for the fifth time that year, destroying a
stone statue of a young man on a horse. Police believed that
one man was responsible for the string of bombings, which
included statues of 18th-century chemist Carl Wilhelm
Scheele, and Sweden's first Social Democratic prime minister, Hjalmar Branting.

POLICE ARRESTED A 51-YEAR-OLD MAN

who bought 10 high-powered rifles, nine 9mm pistols, and
thousands of rounds of ammunition at a K Mart store in
Middleburg Heights, Ohio. After telling the K Mart clerk
"not to come out tonight," he went to another store and
bought $7,000 worth of fabric, saying it was for "covering
up the bodies."

A week before these incidents, police found the same man placing doughnuts on tombstones in a cemetery at night. They said that when asked what he was doing, he told them, "People get hungry." During police questioning after his arrest, he repeatedly said that the world was coming to an end.

WHEN THE LOAN DEPARTMENT AT A SAN

Antonio, Texas, Bank One branch informed a 40-year-old customer that his loan application had been denied, he took off all his clothes, sat down in the office of the vice president for loans, and began to quack. When police arrived, he continued to quack in response to their questions.

GONE BUT NOT FORGOTTEN

• When George Bojarski, 66, died of cancer, his body was taken to a Richmond, Texas, funeral home to be cremated. His son, Larry Bojarski, paid $299 of the $683 cremation bill, but when he failed to pay the balance within three days, workers from the Evans Mortuary dumped the body on the son's porch, nude and covered with a sheet.

• When Mary Hailey Shafer's widower failed to pay the $410 balance due on her $910 tombstone, a work crew from the Catholic-owned Gate of Heaven in Silver Spring, Maryland, went to the cemetery and dug up the granite marker.

• In Santa Ana, California, Joseph de Nobili, 76, filed a breach of contract lawsuit against a mortuary that let his mother's frozen body thaw before he could find a way to preserve it. Lena de Nobili died in 1975 at age 92. Her son, a doctor, spent the next 15 years developing a liquid solution to prevent bacteria growth that causes bodies to decay so he could preserve her in a stainless steel coffin with a hydraulically operated lid that he could open to view her. In the meantime, he kept her body refrigerated at Harbor Lawn-Mount Olive Mortuary. In 1990, while de Nobili was having surgery in Italy, Harbor Lawn workers unplugged the refrigerator his mother was in and shipped the unrefrigerated body to San Diego for burial, explaining that de Nobili hadn't paid the $500 monthly storage fee since 1984. He retrieved her body, which was undamaged because he had already begun bathing it with his solution.

• A woman at Mawuggwe village in Uganda exhumes her husband's corpse every morning and takes it home "to enjoy the sunshine," according to the Kampala *Star*. The paper quoted her as saying her husband, who was buried the previous year, appeared to her in a dream complaining that his grave was chilly and asking to be dug up to lie in the sun. When the corpse is through basking, she returns it to the grave until the next day.

• In Lubbock, Texas, police responding to a complaint by the brother of Wynona Fuller, 64, that his niece Marsha Fuller, 42, was keeping him from seeing his sister, went to the women's apartment and found the mother's decomposing body in bed, covered by a white blanket. After determining that the woman had died of natural causes five months earlier, they questioned the daughter. Sergeant Randy McGuire said Marsha Fuller explained that she had stayed with the body that long because God "had taken her mother's soul out of her body so He could repair it cell by cell," then He would revive her.

• In Romania, three men couldn't afford a hearse to take their dead uncle's body 300 miles from Bucharest to the family graveyard in Caransebes. For about 5 percent of what the hearse would have cost, they bought train tickets for

the four of them, doused their father's body with alcohol to conceal the smell, and told the conductor he was drunk.
• In Kissimmee, Florida, authorities charged live-in caretaker Deborah Josh, 42, with failing to report her 82-year-old employer's death, apparently from natural causes. Instead, according to Osceola County sheriff's Captain Gary Pearce, Josh stored the man's body in a small freezer for two years, explaining that she wanted to continue receiving his monthly pension checks.

AFTER ANNOUNCING "ATTORNEYS HAVE ruined the world" and "now is the day of justice," James Sinclair, 62, shot and killed his lawyer, Michael Friedman, in the Los Angeles County Law Library. He then took his own life.

VOLUNTEER FIREFIGHTER STANLEY KAS- przak, 19, was charged with setting a fire in the storage area of the K Mart where he worked as an assistant manager in Pennsauken, New Jersey. When firefighters from three companies arrived at the scene, they found Kasprzak fully suited in his firefighting outfit. He then led them to the fire.

A YOUNG MAN WHO HAD BEEN DRINKING and sightseeing with friends suddenly yelled "yahoo," then jumped to his death from the 140-foot high Deception Pass Bridge north of Oak Harbor, Washington. His friends said that just prior to the jump they stood on the bridge as the jumper regaled them with tales of his previous jumps from higher places. Witnesses reported seeing the body sucked into a whirlpool.

DURING THE PERSIAN GULF WAR, A

group of 40 foreign journalists was taken prisoner and held by the Iraqis in Baghdad. According to an American photographer, two French photographers in the group demanded that the Iraqis serve them croissants, leaned out of their hotel windows screaming for cigarettes, and berated other journalists for seeming to be friendly with their captors, charging them with collaboration just to get more food.

A MOB OF 10 TO 12 MEN JUMPED AND

beat Carmelo Rivera, 35, while he was walking his dog in the Fordham section of New York City because they mistook him for someone who had struck a woman during a drug deal. Despite the woman's screams that "he didn't do it," the mob continued to beat Rivera to death. His mother said that while her family waited for an ambulance to arrive, a boy knocked on the door to their apartment to deliver an apology from the mob. He explained that they had confused her son with someone else.

HARVARD UNIVERSITY OFFICIALS RE-

ported that a lovesick Austrian student, his advances rejected by a Harvard coed, admitted to placing more than 10,000 harassing trans-Atlantic telephone calls to Harvard students. The Austrian called an average of 10 Harvard students each day, running up a phone bill of more than $30,000.

SCHOOL DAZE

In his first directive after taking the helm as president of
Teikyo Marycrest University in Iowa, Joseph D. Olander
encouraged all students to take a 10- to 15-minute nap
"sometime between 1 and 2 P.M. every day."

THE CONTINUING DESENSITIZING
OF SOCIETY

• When police in Key West, Florida, discovered that the
body of William Everett Delaney, 43, had been lying dead
on his kitchen floor for two months, his 78-year-old roommate told them that he did recall Delaney falling two to
three months earlier, and since then had often asked if he
wanted something to eat or drink or to be taken to the hospital. "He said the guy was very stubborn," Detective Duke
Yannacone explained, "and wouldn't answer him."

Police said that for at least two months the roommate
went about his business, routinely stepping over the body,
which was facedown in the doorway between the kitchen
and bathroom. He also told police that he thought Delaney
was alive because he seemed to change positions and stretch
his legs. Police said that the body had decomposed to the
point that it "seemed to be melting into the floor."
• An 84-year-old woman in Stockholm sat on her balcony for
two and one-half months during the winter before neighbors
realized that she was dead. Police theorized that the woman,
discovered in March, had died while watching New Year's
Eve fireworks. All that time, she was visible sitting on a
chair on the balcony dressed in a hat and coat, her head

leaning against the railing. Neighbor Margaretha Marsellas said that she eventually became suspicious that something was wrong when she noticed the woman sat there around the clock in frigid temperatures.

WHEN JUAN COLON, 19, OF GULF BREEZE,

Florida, went to a doctor complaining of a headache, a CAT scan revealed a bullet lodged in his brain. Colon said that he knew a friend had accidentally shot him above his right ear the day before, but both men thought the bullet had just grazed him. "It felt like it was just a cut until I started throwing up a lot," said Colon.

MARC J. P. CIENKOWSKI, 25, OF BENSA-

lem, Pennsylvania, pleaded guilty to killing Michael Klucznik, 31, by shooting him in the chest with a bow and arrow after an argument over a game of Monopoly. According to Bucks County District Attorney Alan Rubenstein, "The defendant wanted to be the car (game piece) rather than the thimble or hat."

A 56-YEAR-OLD FAYETTE COUNTY, PENN-

sylvania, man was accused of shooting Bernard Danko, 31, when Danko announced that he was leaving a beer-drinking party and taking his keg tap with him. After the shooting, the gunman's son reportedly picked up the bloody tap and placed it back in the keg. Then the father and son and a group of friends, who had gotten together for a day of eating deer meat, drinking beer, and shooting bats, continued to drink while discussing how to dispose of Danko's body.

LAUGH, LAUGH, I THOUGHT I'D DIE

• Police said that Rafael Salvi was standing at a urinal in Miami's Club Rio when a woman chased a man into the men's room and poured a beer on him. Salvi laughed, and the man shot and killed him.

• A singer in a Toronto karaoke club shot two men in the audience, killing one and seriously wounding the other, because they laughed at his singing. "I know it sounds hard to believe," said Detective Sergeant Mike Hamel, "but that appears to be the motive."

HARRISON CITY, PENNSYLVANIA, POLICE

arrested a 61-year-old man for stabbing his 50-year-old wife 219 times. He said that he couldn't stand the way she stocked the refrigerator, piling vegetables in front of the milk.

POLICE IN NEW ORLEANS CHARGED A 37-

year-old man with killing his neighbor Curt King, 42, by stabbing him three times after King cut three inches beyond his property line with a lawn edger.

IT'S TORTURE

• Melyn Richman of Skaneateles, New York, was convicted of menacing and criminal mischief for spray-painting her neighbor George Wolff's face, threatening him with a gun, and heaving a dead raccoon into his car.

• Thinking that he had caught window installer Ronald Henry, 24, stealing, Jeffrey Shephard, 31, stripped him naked, covered him in honey, shot him with a stun gun, and threw him in a pen of Rottweiler puppies. Shephard got three years in jail.

• Enraged over a debt, 33-year-old Mohammed Jabber kidnapped a former Bangladeshi politician in east London, forced a chili pepper up his rectum, and took photos of him writhing in pain. Jabber was jailed for three years.

MANILA POLICE ARRESTED FRANCISCO

Opao, 42, one of 100 flag bearers at the 1992 World Chess Olympiad, because he threatened to impale Philippine President Corazon Aquino on the point of his flagpole.

QUICK, CALL PRESIDENT TRUMAN

ABC News anchor Peter Jennings, reporting during the 1992 Democratic National Convention, identified the Bill Clinton campaign anthem "Don't Stop" (recorded by Fleetwood Mac in 1978) as having been recorded by Jefferson Airplane. Informed of his error the next day, Jennings admitted, "I'm a rock 'n' roll illiterate. I was away during the 1970s in the Mideast. I thought Fleetwood Mac was a car."

LOCK YOUR DOORS

• Convicted serial killer Aileen Wuornos entered a no-contest plea to three murders, explaining, "I hope I'll get

the electric chair as soon as possible. I want to get off this planet."
• New York City police arrested Hamid Raza "Anthony" Bayat, 19, for murdering his father, Mahmoud Bayat, a diamond trader. Hamid cut off his father's head, two middle fingers, and left testicle, beheaded their pet cat and pet parakeet, then tossed his father's head and the cat's torso through a plate-glass window of their 12th floor apartment. Five statues in the apartment had also been beheaded. As he threw down bloody knives and a razor in the apartment lobby, Hamid told a doorman that it was self-defense.
• School officials and fellow students were mystified when 18-year-old Wayne Lo, a violinist, went on a rampage with a semiautomatic weapon at Simon's Rock College in Massachusetts. Lo, who one student described as "anti-everything," killed two and wounded four. He appeared at his arraignment with a shaved head and wearing a sweatshirt bearing the name of the rock group "Sick of It All."
• Eric Houston, 20, who dropped out of Lindhurst High School in Olivehurst, California, returned to his alma mater three years later, took 80 people hostage, shot and killed four, including a history teacher who had flunked him, and wounded 11. During the 8½-hour siege Houston kept repeating, "The school failed me. They left me with a crappy job."
• Joseph Vera, 29, of Victorville, California, was found guilty of animal cruelty for killing and barbecuing his neighbor's collie-pit bull terrier, Astro. Claiming self-defense, Vera explained that the dog attacked him and he hadn't eaten in two days. "I stood over him, looked at him. I saw different types of meals I could make out of him." He went on to describe how he seasoned Astro with salt, pepper, and lemon and proceeded to barbecue his ribs on a grill in his front yard. "I didn't have corn tortillas to make tacos, so I

took the ribs and barbecued the ribs," Vera told the court. The prosecutor charged that Vera killed the dog in revenge for an earlier argument with his neighbor over a VCR. He also pointed out that after the killing, Vera put Astro's head on his neighbor's front gate.

• Serial killer Nathaniel White, charged with killing six women in upstate New York, said that he used a murder scene from the movie *Robocop* as a model for one of his real-life crimes. "I did exactly what I seen in the movie," said White. "When I looked at TV, I would see a movie, and something violent would happen—and it just seems to sink in."

PATRICIA BOUGHTON, WHO SUED ROD

Stewart and two theater owners in Clarkston, Michigan, over a finger injury from a soccer ball the singer kicked into a concert audience, accepted a $17,000 settlement. Her ex-husband, Stephen Boughton, testified that the accident, which permanently disfigured the middle finger of her left hand, helped end their 14-year marriage. "If she hit that hand on something it was all over," he said. "To get into sexual activity, it was very difficult."

A STUDENT AT NORWAY'S OSLO UNIVER-

sity filed a lawsuit against the school to let him take examinations. The 39-year-old astrophysics student, who enrolled in the university when he was 21, lives in a cave and wears torn and dirty clothes to class. "He has been banned from taking exams since 1981 because the university says his body and clothes smell so bad that he cannot sit in a room with other students," said his lawyer, Peter Graver, who explained that his client also wants the university to pay $470,000.

SMOKE 'EM IF YOU GOT 'EM

• Despite attempts by his friend to pull him from the path of an oncoming train, Jeffrey Scott Jackson, 30, refused to get up until he had finished rolling a cigarette. The train was unable to stop and Jackson, still rolling his cigarette, was struck and killed.

• When administrators at Saanich Peninsula Hospital in Victoria, British Columbia, decided to enforce regional anti-smoking laws, they told extended-care patient Lionel Thomas, 80, that he would have to take his smoke breaks outside. A month later, he died of pneumonia, prompting his daughter, Vicki Whyte, to blame the administrators. "I don't think my dad had a long life in front of him," she said, "but this shortened it."

• Edward Brown, 22, walked into a New York City grocery and paid 40 cents for two loose cigarettes. One of the dimes rolled off the counter and out of reach, so store owner Gabriel Azcona demanded 10 more cents from Brown. As the two began arguing, another patron stepped in, paid the dime, and lit Brown's cigarette. Brown reportedly became angry that Azcona was taking too long in handing over a book of matches and blew smoke in Azcona's face. Azcona then pulled a gun and shot Brown dead.

• Authorities blamed a half-hour rampage by two club-wielding patients at the Clifton T. Perkins Hospital Center for the criminally insane in Jessup, Maryland, on the hospital's new smoking ban. The patients tore legs off a heavy table in a maximum security ward and smashed several light fixtures before striking two ward orderlies and two security guards. "It's a volatile place," Michael Golden, a spokesperson for the state health department, conceded, "and the patients have a history of acting out their aggressions in a violent way. The smoking policy may have been just one of several concerns that these people had."

DESPITE BEING PAID $2.9 MILLION A

year, baseball player Jack Clark filed for bankruptcy midway through a three-year contract because of what his lawyer termed "expensive hobbies." According to his Chapter 7 bankruptcy petition, filed in Orange County, California, Clark collected some 20 automobiles, several residences, and a drag-racing team while falling $6.67 million in debt. The erstwhile slugger, who at the time of the filing four months into the 1992 season was batting .211 with four home runs and 29 runs batted in, blamed his money problems for distracting him from baseball.

A PLAN BY THE ISRAELI ARMY TO BOOST

the morale of its soldiers by encouraging family involvement backfired. Noting that some families went so far as to join the tail end of 55-mile endurance marches and help their exhausted offspring reach the finish, Major General Ran Goren, chief of human resources, said discipline was being undermined by "excessive interference and pampering by parents."

HAIR TODAY, GONE TOMORROW

• A South Korean university student, identified only by his family name, Yang, killed himself by jumping from a 150-foot building in Inchon. Police explained that Yang had been worried about losing his hair.

• Los Angeles police charged an 18-year-old man with burning down two barber shops and vandalizing a third because he didn't like the way they cut his hair.

• A jury in Palm Beach County, Florida, awarded Missy Freshour, 33, $2,500 for her humiliating hairdo. She claimed that she went to a beauty salon to have her shoulder-length hair frosted, but instead it fell out by the handful, requiring her to have it cut like a boy's to cover thin spots.

• In Alhambra, California, police charged a 19-year-old man with fatally stabbing his 58-year-old father. According to Rosalee Rubio, the two argued over the haircut she gave him. The father wanted his son's hair long like his own, but the teenager wanted a Marine-style haircut.

RICHARD REDD, 46, THE LAWYER FOR THE

Baton Rouge, Louisiana, police department, was charged with malfeasance in office for asking exotic dancers and professional escorts to bare their breasts when they applied to him for the $25 licenses the city required for people in their line of work.

DURING A BEAUTY PAGEANT TO PICK THE

Dominican Republic's representative to the Miss Universe and Miss World pageants, contestant Julie Ramirez, 22, removed the top portion of her bathing suit and proceeded to

waltz topless for the national television audience. Other contestants said that when Ramirez returned to the dressing
room afterward, she argued with the other contestants and
threatened to return to the stage completely nude.

COLOMBIAN POLICE ARRESTED A WOMAN
at the Bogota airport bound for Miami after noting her "dis-
proportionately large" buttocks, which, according to the police communique, had been surgically implanted with eight
bags containing one pound of heroin each.

OFFICIALS ACCUSED MEMBERS OF THE
Merced County, California, grand jury investigating the
county's child dependency system of plagiarizing a report
issued by a grand jury in San Diego County. They concluded
that as much as three-fourths of the Merced report came
from the San Diego report, including some of the testimony.

KAVIN PEEPLES, 29, AN INMATE AT THE
Southern Ohio Correctional Facility near Lucasville, said
that he killed fellow prisoner Ronald McCaman, 43, at the
urging of a demon. Said Peeples, "So I wake up at 2 o'clock
in the morning, and this thing tells me that this is a good
day, everything's going to be just great, put on a happy face,
and we're going to kill McCaman at 8 o'clock." After stran-
gling McCaman, Peeples said, "I sort of felt like . . . the
whole world had been remade. I came to the conclusion that
God had condoned my actions."

DURING THE MIDDLE OF THEIR INTERRO-

gation of Manjit Singh, 30, arrested in connection with the 1985 bombing of an Air India jet, police heard a crunching sound and saw blood coming out of the prisoner's mouth. Singh, a top-ranking Sikh terrorist, had chewed off his own tongue to avoid answering their questions.

AN EDENSBURG, PENNSYLVANIA, JURY

convicted 35-year-old Rickie Gaddis of multiple counts of child abuse, finding him guilty of beating, burning, and cutting his children to drink their blood. The children testified at the trial that Gaddis cut their fingers and collected the blood to use in a ritual to bring their deceased sister back from the dead.

A 16-YEAR-OLD WHO SHOT TWO PEOPLE IN

a Kansas City jewelry store holdup used money from the heist to pay library book fines at his high school. Just before the robbery occurred the teenager had been informed that he owed $30.15 in fines, including $15.40 for the volume *Legacy of Freedom*.

A 14-YEAR-OLD BOY WALKED UP TO THE

drive-in window of the First Virginia Bank in Crofton, Virginia, pulled a handgun part of the way out of his pocket and demanded a lollipop from the teller. According to police, the boy said, "Give me a pop or I will shoot you." The teller handed over the candy and the boy walked off. He was later arrested and turned over to his mother.

PET THEORIES

• San Franciscan Steven Lightfoot, 28, convinced that author Stephen King actually killed John Lennon, painted a statement across his van, parked in downtown Bangor, Maine, King's hometown. The sign proclaimed, "Photos prove it's Stephen King, not Mark David Chapman, getting John Lennon's autograph. No joke, folks."

• In an attempt to make the point that crime fighting in the Netherlands had grown lax, a 33-year-old man took a hammer and went on a rampage, smashing 150 windows in the Interior and Justice ministries, causing about $600,000 worth of damage.

• Larry Moor, 45, a snake handler who founded the British Columbia Association of Reptile Owners to teach the proper handling of snakes and dispel fear and misunderstanding of the animals, died after being bitten by his pet Egyptian cobra.

IN SANTA CRUZ, CALIFORNIA, PROSECU- tors accused former roller-coaster operator Deborah Jean Finch, 20, of being a vampire who killed a neighbor and drank his blood.

AT A CONCERT IN WARWICK, RHODE IS- land, singer Patti LaBelle was 90 minutes into her performance when she stopped singing, complained to the audience that the seafood platter she had been served backstage before the show contained only seven shrimp, then walked off the stage.

AFTER LIVING IN A TREE FOR FIVE YEARS

in Pankshin, Nigeria, then disappearing for two weeks, Michael Balama, 45, reappeared in a nearby tree. He climbs down to lower branches to get food prepared by his wife, who said the thing she missed most about the father of nine living in trees "is that we can no longer make love together and produce more children."

LOVE HURTS

• Upset that a romance had soured, Ge Ruiwang, a Chinese stone worker, attempted to rig a dynamite booby trap in the explosives storeroom at work, where he hoped to lure his ex-girlfriend and her family. Instead, due to an error with the trigger mechanism, Ge was killed in a small blast as he left the site. Then police investigators arriving at the scene set off a trip-wire that ignited 2.5 tons of dynamite, killing eight more people.

• Police in Amherst, New York, said that a 34-year-old man, trying to burn down his girlfriend's apartment, threw a fire-bomb through the wrong window, starting a fire that killed a man and his three-year-old son.

• Upset that his girlfriend broke up with him, Randy Mock, 30, of Edmonton, Canada, flew his Cessna aircraft around her neighborhood for two hours, demanding that she talk with him, until the plane ran out of fuel. He then crashed into her house. Mock was hospitalized with head injuries.

• William Marconda, 22, of Fontana, California, had to be rescued from the burning wreckage of a small plane he was piloting after it crashed onto a residential street. Police suspected that Marconda stole the plane and tried to crash it into the home of his estranged wife.

WHEN BUDGET CUTS FORCED A GRAND

Junction, Colorado, suicide prevention hot line to close, callers were referred to a 900 number costing 25 cents for the first minute and $2.50 a minute after that.

IN TAMPA, FLORIDA, CIRCUIT COURT

Judge Daniel Gallagher ordered a three-year-old German shepherd named Hitler to be put to death for biting three people, noting, "One person said, 'With a name like that, he's got to be bad.'"

LOS ANGELES POLICE ARRESTED A 26-

year-old black man, for flying into a rage at a dinner party and attacking his white hosts. He tried to choke Suzzanne Lissete, 21, and managed to slash Laura Freed, 32, with a knife, according to Ted Goldstein of the City Attorney's Office, explaining that "it turned ugly" during dinner chitchat when the man learned the women's black cat was named "Nigger."

BASKETBALL ALL-STAR CHARLES BAR-

kley of the Phoenix Suns charged that he was misquoted in a new book about him. The book was his autobiography.

A 57-YEAR-OLD WOMAN FOUND BY THE

crew of a coal train lying on the tracks outside Price, Utah, explained that she had fallen from Amtrak's California Zephyr, bound from Chicago to San Francisco, while looking for a restroom. Officials said the train was going about 35 mph when the woman apparently fell from a side door. She lay injured on the tracks for more than 12 hours in near-freezing temperatures. According to Utah Highway Patrol Sergeant Billie Hunt, the woman told rescuers that she asked two deer hunters who happened by for help, but one said, "I don't think there's anything we can do for her," and left.

HEY LARRY! HEY MOE!

• An explosion killed 10 people and injured 10 others in a miners' dormitory in China's Guangdong province after a burning candle fell onto 53 pounds of explosives and detonators that one miner kept stored in his room.

• Chinese soldiers detonated 12,000 tons of dynamite in Paotai Mountain to level a hill for expansion of an airport. Although the government announced that measures were in place to buffer the magnitude of the blast to only 2.5 on the Richter scale, the explosion, said to be the world's largest non-nuclear one, triggered an earthquake registering 3.4. Tremors were felt 27 miles away in Hong Kong, and windows rattled in Macao, 18 miles away.

• Teenagers holding a late-night beer party at a Chevron oil tank in Grayson County, Texas, set off an explosion that killed one person and injured four. Four of the young men reportedly climbed on top of the tank, opened its top, and tried to look inside it. Hampered by the dark, one apparently leaned over the opening and lit a match or lighter.

• According to Mercer County, West Virginia, sheriff's Deputy L. R. Catron, a 38-year-old man shot himself three times in his right foot, each shot coming from a separate gun he was cleaning at one sitting. The man, who had been drinking beer, explained that when his .32-caliber handgun fired it didn't hurt, so he finished and began cleaning his .38-caliber gun. The deputy quoted the man as saying that the second round "stung a little, but not too bad." Only after he was shot by his .357-caliber pistol did he call an ambulance. That shot "really hurt," the man said, "because the bullet was a hollow point."

MATTHEW GARDNER EXPLAINED THAT HE

falsely confessed to setting several fires' in the hopes that he would be sent to prison instead of the Utah State Hospital where he claimed he was denied caffeinated coffee. Gardner's therapist told District Judge Anne Stirba, "[Gardner] has a strong dislike to being served decaffeinated coffee." Salt Lake City police suspected that Gardner set three small fires at a home for the elderly and handicapped because the facility served him decaf during an interview and then denied him residency there.

NEIGHBORHOOD WEIRDOS (FIRST IN A CONTINUING SERIES)

Seven years after Cloyd Ferrall Howard left on a "suicide walk," the Jefferson County, Colorado, Sheriff's Department identified his remains, found by hikers in a wilderness area. Police, who discovered Howard fully skeletonized, lying on his back above a scenic vista, theorized that a nearby eagle's nest kept small animals from scattering the body. The skeleton was still wearing hiking boots, jeans, a jean jacket, and a digital watch, and his pocket held 80 cents in change, none of the coins dated past 1982. Police say that Howard clearly intended to kill himself by exposure to the cold since temperatures were below freezing on the day he disappeared.

Howard, a self-described psychic researcher, had at one time been run out of Central City, Colorado, by fellow residents fearful of his home-installed "Frankenstein laboratory." "Everybody in town talked about the fact that Howard had this strange electronic experimental stuff in his

house," said a former deputy marshal who investigated
Howard back in the early 1970s. "He experimented on his
wife. People who were in and out of that house constantly
were all weirdos."

When his first wife was arrested for drunk driving in
1971, she committed suicide in her cell after having been
jailed only 10 minutes. According to a report in the *Denver
Post*, Howard also claimed to have done exorcism work for
the Universal Church of the Masters in Boulder. "We put
the material they bring in—herbs, spices, and some saliva
from the person who has entities within him—into a cardboard box," he said. "I put it in a chamber in the polarizing
unit, and this forms an electro-psychic link from the material
to the person." The former deputy marshal described walking through Howard's house as being "like I walked through
the gate into another world—another place, another world.
I was not myself, I felt very strange. Things I had never
felt before in my life. I even felt this guy thinking about
me."

THE CITY OF OMAHA, NEBRASKA, AN-
nounced that its $10,000 gun amnesty program would pay
$50 for every real gun turned in and $1 for every toy gun.
"Guns, real and toy, are a danger to our community when
they are used in the wrong way," Mayor P. J. Morgan said.
"With the toy-gun amnesty, we are trying to instill a knowledge that guns and violence have no place in our
community."

IN KENMORE, NEW YORK, A 30-YEAR-OLD
man tried to kill himself by taking a running leap through
a closed fourth-story window. He survived by landing on a

car 40 feet below, buckling the roof and doors and smashing its rear windows. Witnesses told police that the man, dazed and bleeding from facial cuts, then strode back into the building, rode the elevator to the fourth floor, and repeated his suicide attempt by leaping from the same window. He landed on the same car and survived, although police Captain Emil Palombo explained that the man was more seriously injured in the second fall because the car no longer absorbed the impact and "kind of flattened out like a dumpster." Palombo did observe that "other than a broken wrist and a broken ankle, he's in as good a shape as you or I."

IN 1992, LLOYD'S OF LONDON ANNOUNCED

the worst loss in the insurer's 304-year history: $3.8 billion.

RALPH KRAMDEN, CALL YOUR OFFICE

• Therese Jean Perry, 20, stole a bus from a depot in Sydney, Australia, and drove about picking up passengers. Asked why, she explained, "Because I thought I was a bus driver."
• A female bus passenger in Houston, tired of waiting for the driver to return from a coffee break, commandeered the bus and drove several blocks. "The bus driver took a long time coming," she said, "so I did the next best thing." Asked why she stopped, she replied, "I think we ran out of gas."
• Ann Smith, 38, of Rotherham, England, left her husband after nine months of marriage due to what she felt was his unusual obsession with buses. Mark Smith, 29, took his new bride on a tour of bus garages on their honeymoon, became

angry when she neglected to clean his collection of 36,000 bus photos, and crashed Ann's car while he was looking at a bus, sending her to the hospital with head injuries.

A MAN IDENTIFIED ONLY AS RAJU EN-

tered the bear pen at the Karachi, Pakistan, zoo and challenged the animals to a fight. Three bears mauled him.

APPARENTLY DISSATISFIED AFTER TALK-

ing to high school administrators about a dispute between his son and another student, a Centreville, Virginia, man marched down to the school cafeteria and punched the other boy himself.

NIPPLE-SUCKING TOURISTS ROBBED
(Guaranteed Actual Headline Used)

Police in Bangkok arrested a gang of transvestites after Syrian and Hong Kong tourists complained that the gang first lured them to suck their nipples, then robbed them. The nipples had been covered with tranquilizers to put the victims to sleep. Transvestite Somboom Wannasut explained that while it's common for such gangs to doctor drinks for tourists, "many of our customers did not drink, so we would get them to suck our drug-laced nipples."

THE CITY OF HOLLYWOOD, FLORIDA,

found itself facing a $3.8-million bill for a computer system that city officials have no idea how to program. An auditor's report explained that even if the city could figure out how to program the computer, it probably would be obsolete by then.

IN DISASTER'S WAKE

• Allen and Bea Bernkrant filed a lawsuit against the Radisson Suite Hotel in Boca Raton, Florida, charging that the hotel stole 20 towels from their room. The couple explained that they checked in after Hurricane Andrew knocked out their home's electricity, bringing with them a 50-pound bag of towels they had used to sop up water blown through their French doors. Bea Bernkrant said that she planned to wash the towels, but they disappeared.

• After Hurricane Andrew hit Florida, the Federal Emergency Management Agency spent $50,000 on billboards to improve its image and $73,000 on polo shirts for staff members. The agency also asked for bids for buttons and Frisbees printed with its 800 number.

• Soon after Andrew hit south Louisiana, the business editor of the *Pacific Daily News* in Guam phoned *The Times-Picayune* in New Orleans for a damage report. John McCarthy explained that he called specifically on behalf of readers who were worried that shipments of Tabasco hot sauce from the bayou region might be interrupted.

RUSSIAN TEENAGER VITALY KLIMAKHIN,

who dropped out of high school to become a writer, finished his first book in 107 days. It consisted of the word "Ford" written 400,000 times. "My work is able to provoke a whole range of emotions in people," he said. "Some think it is just stupid. Others take it a bit more seriously."

WHEN KLAUS MATTHIESEN, ENVIRON-

ment minister of the German state of North Rhine Westphalia, condemned daily showers as a threat to the environment because they use water and heat unnecessarily, special interest groups reacted swiftly. "Not taking a shower every day in the summer would be crazy," said Hans Joachim Keller, president of the German Public Health Movement. Achim Tilmes of the German Bath Society added: "Some people even need to shower twice a day."

IN FLORIDA, DEMOCRAT ERIC ADAM KAP-

lan, 28, withdrew from the race for the state legislature after police charged him with firing five shots into the home of his opponent. Judith Starks, wife of Republican state Representative Robert Starks, was shot in the leg while she slept. Prior to the incident, Seminole County Democratic Party officials had criticized Kaplan for mounting a lackluster campaign against Starks in the heavily Republican district. "He's done no advertising," volunteer Stan Stevens explained. "He hasn't done anything. We've been giving him hell for not getting going."

PENNSYLVANIA SUPREME COURT JUSTICE

Rolf Larsen reported that he was nearly struck by an automobile "commandeered" by his colleague, Justice Stephen A. Zappala. Larsen said that only a passerby's warning saved him from Zappala's "apparent attempt" to run him down.

CITING STILL-SECRET WHITE HOUSE

tapes, *The New Yorker* magazine reported in December 1992 that during the 1972 election, President Nixon favored planting campaign literature for his opponent, Senator George McGovern, in the apartment of the man arrested for shooting Alabama Governor George Wallace. The magazine also quoted White House counsel Charles Colson as saying the idea to link suspect Arthur Bremer to the McGovern campaign after the May 15 attempted assassination got as far as approaching E. Howard Hunt about flying to Milwaukee, where Bremer lived. The magazine said that the plan was abandoned because the FBI moved too quickly to seal off Bremer's apartment, causing Nixon to complain "about the missed opportunity to damage McGovern."

NEATNESS COUNTS

• In Westminster, California, Keven Vincent Condon, 36, shot himself to death after calling 911 and pinning a sign to the front door of his mobile home that said, "dead body inside, call coroner, attempt suicide." Inside police found a fresh pot of coffee waiting for them and the victim's body lying on several plastic body bags carefully spread across his bed. A completed death certificate was on top of his night stand. Police said that Condon, a former mortuary worker who used to pick up bodies from the coroner's office, apparently wanted to make things easy on the officers and coroner's deputies who would be handling his case.

• In Lakewood, Colorado, Rich Masters, 57, and his wife Jaime, 49, shot themselves to death after mowing the lawn and cleaning the house, then leaving a note in the mailbox instructing the letter carrier to call the sheriff's office. Also inside the mailbox were a portable telephone so the carrier could make the call and $50 "for your trouble." The note included instructions on how to enter the house, where to find them, and what family members to call. Inside, they placed their driver's licenses and other papers in a conspicuous place. Then they spread a quilt, blanket, and shower curtain on the couch so it wouldn't be stained when they sat on it and shot themselves.

2
News from the Twilight Zone

DETROIT RESIDENT JAMES BLAKELY FILED suit against the *Detroit Free Press* and *Detroit News*, demanding the papers drop their syndicated horoscopes and pay him $9 million for the suffering that astrology has caused him. Noting that horoscopes destroyed his marriage and have caused "an enormous amount of problems" in his life, the 19-page handwritten lawsuit contended that horoscopes are a consumer fraud and the devil's work because they predict events that will not occur.

SELF-PROCLAIMED WITCH KARLYN STRA- ganana of Antioch, California, demanded that the Mount Diablo School District ban the fairy tale "Hansel and Gretel" because it teaches children that it is acceptable to kill witches. Straganana's complaint followed a mock trial by fifth-graders at a West Pittsburg school that found the children in the Grimm Brothers story acted in self-defense when they murdered the witch. Noting that the tale depicts witches as child-eating monsters, Straganana said that the school "would not use a story that would put any other religion in a light like this."

IN ITALY, A WOMAN JUDGED TO HAVE
Italy's most beautiful legs was disqualified from competing in the Miss Italy pageant after officials discovered that she was born a man. Giovanna Fanelli, 27, born Gianni Fanelli, had both male and female sex organs until undergoing an operation a year earlier to remove the male organ.

LORNE AND CASSANDRA COOPER ABAN-
doned their 11-year-old daughter along a rural Virginia highway "with no shoes, a blanket, a couple of Bibles and some of the mother's journals," according to state Trooper D. P. Whittemore, because she wouldn't join them in committing suicide. He explained that the girl, her five-year-old brother, mother, and stepfather were returning from a visit with Cassandra Cooper's aunt and uncle at New Heritage USA, the South Carolina resort founded by convicted evangelist Jim Bakker. The parents began talking about a suicide pact and asked the daughter "if she would go with them to heaven but she said no," Whittemore said. "Then they asked the little boy if he wanted to go with the sister or go with them to heaven." When the boy told them he wanted to go with them, "they put the little girl out on the side of the road on the interstate."

After a minister who was driving by rescued the girl, police apprehended the Coopers 60 miles away. At a hearing before their trial, Sharon Powers, Cassandra Cooper's aunt, testified that the Coopers told her they had been fasting and praying all week and "they had made a new discovery and they wanted to share it with us." They talked for about an hour, although Powers said, "I couldn't actually tell you what they talked about because what they said didn't make any sense." The Coopers' daughter added that during the trip, her stepfather had been talking about a dog, his grand-father, and singer Eric Clapton's son, all of whom are dead.

AUTHORITIES IN SULLIVAN COUNTY, NEW

York, issued littering tickets to rabbi Issac Ginsberg, 65, for dumping thousands of leaflets from a helicopter heralding the coming of the Messiah.

A 22-YEAR-OLD CHINESE MAN, IDENTIFIED

as Wei, was so sure that he had mastered the mystical art of "qi gong" that he announced he would stop a speeding locomotive to demonstrate his powers. Outside Shanghai, he stretched out on the tracks in front of a speeding freight train and tried to stop it. He failed and was crushed to death beneath the cow-catcher in front of the locomotive's wheels.

ODD ENDINGS

• Gordon Crops, a British test pilot who headed an eight-member team seeking the wreckage of a Thai airliner that crashed into a mountain in the Himalayas, died of altitude sickness.

• Wuyi Pan, 42, an instructor at New Mexico Tech married to a graduate student who conducted lightning research, was killed while walking on campus during a storm when he was struck by lightning.

• Marshall Gambrell, 25, was killed while on his way to visit relatives in Connecticut, police said, when he lost control of his car in Hamden, crashed into a cemetery, and was hurled from the car into a marble headstone.

• Tess Elliott, 23, one of 11 semifinalists in the 1992 Miss USA pageant, who said that she learned to skydive to overcome her fear of heights, died in a parachuting accident seven months after the pageant.

DESPERATE TO IMPROVE CROP YIELDS,

the Russian Agriculture Ministry invited "the nation's leading psychics, magicians, and representatives of small enterprises that deal with weather control" to a conference, according to *Komsomolskaya Pravda*. Unfortunately, the paper reported, Agriculture Minister Viktor Khlystun "expressed dissatisfaction that the psychics, magicians, and weather controllers are acting in an uncoordinated manner, causing thunderstorms and rain at random sites."

BULGARIA'S CUSTOMS SERVICE RE-

ported that 90 of its officers had been trained in extrasensory perception to stop smugglers. Authorities explained that officers trained in ESP confiscated more contraband than their colleagues who rely on conventional methods.

MORE THAN 20 BUSINESS LEADERS

from the Norwegian town of Seljord traveled to Scotland in summer 1992 to study how the region around Loch Ness has marketed its legendary lake monster as a lucrative attraction, generating $42 million in tourism around the town of Inverness. Seljord revealed that it has its own elusive giant sea serpent and hopes, according to Rune Handlykken of the Seljord Trade Association, to develop its "monster tradition into a tourist activity and build up the identity of the town."

Meanwhile, an 85-foot Norwegian vessel began plying the waters of Loch Ness, using computers, underwater cameras, and depth-finding sonar to discover whether Nessie exists. The cost of the three-year, high-technology research effort was put at $5 million.

THE WOMEN'S BIBLE COMMENTARY, A

compilation of the wisdom of "40 of the world's foremost female biblical experts," offered its own version of the story of Adam and Eve. Eve is no longer "easy prey" for a dissembling snake. Her decision to take the apple is seen as a conscious act that brought her and her family knowledge and culture. Adam, on the other hand, is seen as rather limp in the feminist interpretation. "He takes the fruit from Eve without question," and when God accuses him of disobedience, he blames her.

IN BROOKLYN, THIEVES BROKE THROUGH

a chain link fence at St. Edmund's Church and stole a 3-foot, 100-pound marble statue of St. Bernadette. Associate pastor Robert Romano said that he had no idea why anyone would steal it, noting it had only one devotee and "it's not worth anything. The only thing you could use it for is a lawn ornament."

THE MYSTERIOUS CURSE OF THE PHA-

raohs is real, according to Egyptian scientist Sayeed Mohammed Thebat, who blamed the mysterious deaths of many people entering previously unopened tombs on radioactivity. Thebat, a medical professor at Cairo University, said the radioactivity was released by an unidentified substance used in the mummification process more than 3,000 years ago, then built up inside the tombs for centuries to hazardous levels.

CLAIMING THAT TRANSCENDENTAL MEDI-

tation is at least partially responsible for the breakup of the Soviet Union, Maharishi Mahesh Yogi offered his help to other places that really need it, like Los Angeles. He announced that if 1,000 people would meditate daily for 90 minutes each morning and evening, the city's residents would experience a peaceful and harmonious environment and freedom from crime. He explained that his plan to bring harmony to Los Angeles would cost $2.8 million to hire 1,000 positive-meditators and gather them in one place to emit positive waves. He added that for about $20 million he could gather 7,000 meditators and bring harmony to the whole world.

Meanwhile, the maharishi and magician Doug Henning announced that they were seeking backers for their billion-dollar theme park, called Maharishi Veda Land. They said they had already bought 450 acres for the park beside Walt Disney World in Orlando.

SIGN, SIGN, EVERYWHERE A SIGN

Police in Windham Township, New York, found the body of God. Diane S. God, 37, who had been shot by an unknown assailant, was pronounced dead by Bradford County coroner Eugene Farr.

MARCOS ANTONIO BONILLA, A BEARDED

man dressed in a long white tunic and army boots, who spends his time among the slum dwellers of Managua, Nicaragua, proclaimed that he is Jesus, the son of God, "the same who was here 2,000 years ago. The same spirit exactly." Hundreds of people have flocked to his home in the barrio to hear him preach his message of peace and to be cured of various afflictions. Bonilla, who has a wife and three children, was born in 1958 and used to be a teacher and handyman until he received a message from God to go public following a solar eclipse. He urges compassion for the poor who he said "have been forgotten by the whole world." Nicaragua's cardinal, Miguel Obando y Bravo, refused a request for an audience with Bonilla, saying that he is a nut and that "Jesus has already come and gone."

YOSHIHIKO OTSUKE, A PHYSICS PROFES-

sor at Japan's Waseda University, accused Japanese subway officials of keeping secret the discovery of many sets of concentric circles appearing in the dust on the walls and floor of a Japanese subway tunnel. Otsuke said that the rings, three inches in diameter, were caused by "plasma generated in the air" and that the tunnels create conditions much like his own plasma generator. He also believes plasma to be behind England's mysterious crop circles.

IN 1992, FOR THE SECOND CONSECUTIVE

year, two large doughnut-shaped circles appeared in a field near Troy, Illinois. Peter Bostrom, a nearby landowner who documented the appearance of the 40-foot and 35-foot circles both years, brought a number of scientists to the site to investigate. W. C. Levengood, a biophysicist, said that he found structural changes in microscopic pits in the cell walls of the plants that had been depressed to form the circles. Levengood said that he could only reproduce those changes by treating the plants with a rapid burst of heat in a microwave oven. Sherry Yarkosky, a chemist, said that the plants revealed sodium levels twice as high as untouched plants nearby and a 5 percent decrease in nitrogen content.

Said Bostrom, "Everyone I've talked to has been unable to find any evidence that these circles are a natural occurrence. Everyone says there has been some kind of energy applied here that has pushed these plants down in such a uniform way, all radiating out from the center. They are not just lying down and dying."

IN MAY 1992, THE AREA AROUND ST.

Paul, Minnesota, experienced a number of frightening clown sightings in which a man dressed as a clown engaged in window peeping and flashed a knife at some children. In one incident the clown was described as wearing a green-and-white bow tie, while in another he was said to be wearing an orange fuzzy wig, red spots on his cheeks, and a smile face painted on a white background. A graduation ceremony for a clown class at Lakewood Community College, coming

in the midst of the media reports, further scared people who witnessed the graduating class in their costumes. One clown who stopped in a store on her way to the ceremony was told, "We don't like clowns. We don't want you around anymore." The mystery clown was never found, but numerous local professional clowns felt that he was ruining their reputation.

IN THE EARLY MORNING HOURS OF DE-

cember 5, 1991, an unknown object with a diameter of 2 to 11 yards passed by the Earth at a distance of 290,000 miles. Its brightness fluctuated at a rate of almost once a minute, suggesting that it was a man-made object, perhaps something such as one of the original rockets used between 1968 and 1972 during an Apollo mission. However, nothing in the launch records of the Jet Propulsion laboratory could account for its identity. No known asteroid possesses the circular orbit that it exhibited. It disappeared during the point of its closest approach to our planet.

On August 10 of that same year, astronauts aboard a space shuttle flight sighted a curved object about the size and shape of a car bumper. According to NASA, it was at least the third time that the object had been seen by shuttle astronauts.

MAYBE THEY KNOW SOMETHING WE DON'T

On March 19, 1992, the mission bells rang in San Juan Capistrano, California, to signal the annual return of the swallows from South America. However, bird watchers in attendance reported only the arrival of a white-throated swift and a hummingbird. Locals said that development in the area has displaced the birds' food supply, and they are now returning to marshlands in Irvine.

*ACCORDING TO A REPORT IN JACK ANDER-*son's column, about 20 American teenagers, many the children of military personnel attending the Defense Department-run Curundu Junior High in Panama, were members of a Satanic cult who were planning a mass suicide before they were found out. The teenagers, aged 13 to 15, had conducted blood rituals, cutting their bodies to exchange blood for the suicide pact and killing small animals on the Air Force base there. After parents intervened to thwart the suicide plan, the U.S. military broke up the cult, hospitalizing some teens and reassigning some families to other postings in the United States.

POLICE IN CHINA STEPPED IN TO PREVENT

more than 100 followers of Xiong Chenhua, a peasant woman who proclaimed the imminent end of the world, from participating in a mass suicide. Many of the followers, who were prepared to drink poisoned liquor, were found kneeling on the ground, waiting for Xiong to return from a meeting with Jesus.

EVANGELICAL MINISTER RAMON MORA-

les Almazan urged his parishioners to remain with him in his church even as they were overcome by toxic fumes from a 30- by 15-foot butane gas lamp ignited for a late-night ceremony in the Mount of Olives church in El Charquillo, Mexico. Police found 30 bodies. There were only three survivors, who told state police that when people started choking on the fumes, Almazan urged them to stay calm, assuring them that "God was drawing near."

GET ME REDDY KILL-O-WATT!

• Reports out of the Italian village of San Gottardo claimed that numerous plastic objects in several homes were inexplicably catching fire. In at least five houses, light bulbs, light switches, a wheelchair seat cover, and a moped fender, all plastic, ignited and melted. Technicians from the state electricity authority, sent to investigate, witnessed the plastic parts of their instruments melt before their eyes. At the time some experts suggested that the strange heat may somehow have been generated by excess electricity produced by high-power generators at a U.S. communications base near the town.

• The China Youth News reported the strange case of four-year-old Tong Tangjiang, a boy whose body spontaneously ignited and burned through his clothes. Tong was hospitalized after his grandmother saw smoke pouring from his pants. Within two hours doctors saw him ignite four times, burning his right hand, armpits, and private parts. The newspaper claimed that Tong was the first case of spontaneous combustion discovered in China and said that doctors detected a strong electric current running through his body.

BIOLOGISTS COUNTING FISH FROM A

two-seat submarine 690 feet below the surface of the ocean 20 miles west of Baranof Island off the coast of Alaska in September 1989, viewed a sunken Holstein cow out their porthole. Biologist Tory O'Connell from the Alaska Department of Fish and Game, along with the sub's pilot, viewed and videotaped the cow for several seconds. A reporter from the *Sitka Sentinel*, sent to view the videotape, concurred that it did appear to be a cow. Apart from the fact that the condition of the cow suggested that it hadn't been there long, no one could offer any theories as to how it got there.

SINCE 1983, HUNDREDS OF SHEEP IN EX-

moor, a desolate area 200 miles west of London, have been savagely killed by a mystery animal, which has come to be called the Beast of Exmoor. Despite numerous searches over the 260-square-mile moor, some conducted by the British marines, nothing has been found. While several inves-

tigators are convinced that the attacks are the work of pumas (a species of big cat not indigenous to England), others are just as certain that the beast's padmarks, extraordinary leaping ability, and blood-sucking habits (the sheep have been torn apart and most of the blood sucked from their bodies) suggest that the beast is something else entirely.

FOR MONTHS AFTER HURRICANE HUGO

devastated the Carolinas in 1990, a photograph that was purported to have been taken at the height of the storm circulated among the populace. It showed an image many saw as a robed figure standing with its arms outstretched amid storm clouds. The Wal-Mart in Gastonia, North Carolina, sold more than 1,000 reprints of the photo at $1.47 each for a 5- by 7-inch or 28 cents for wallet size. While many believed that it was a photo of Jesus, Kevin Moran, an expert on the Shroud of Turin, said, "It's a picture we've seen many, many times before. It was made in a darkroom." One woman claimed to have seen the same photo 15 to 20 years earlier in Pennsylvania.

IN EARLY 1992 ISRAEL WAS HIT BY THREE

snowstorms, each termed "once-in-a-generation" events, which buried the northern sections of the country under more than four feet of snow, the most winter precipitation ever recorded. One of the storms cut the 80-mile-long rope, known as the Eruv, which surrounds the city of Jerusalem and symbolically turns the whole city into a single dwelling unit for the ultra-Orthodox Jews living inside it. The rope thus creates a situation that exempts them from violating the Sabbath by carrying anything outside of one's home.

Rabbi Yehoshua Pollack, deputy head of the Jerusalem Religious Council, warned that until the rope was repaired, the tens of thousands of ultra-Orthodox Jews living in the city would be forbidden from walking with young children in carriages or even carrying food outside of their houses.

Later that year, a Hasidic Jewish community of Lubavitchers living in southern Florida faxed their spiritual leader, Rabbi Menachem Schneerson in Brooklyn, and asked him if they should comply with evacuation orders in the advent of Hurricane Andrew. The rabbi told them all to ignore the warnings and to sit tight. Of the 25 Lubavitcher institutions in Florida, 15 were directly in the path of the hurricane. After Andrew hit, the Lubavitchers and their property were all intact.

YOU ARE GETTING SLEEPY

• A bank cashier in the southern Italian city of Reggio Calabria told police that a robber hypnotized her into handing over $4,000.

• More than a year earlier, a gang operating in the Italian port city of Brindisi hypnotized numerous shopkeepers before robbing their stores. In one incident, police saw the gang place a cashier in a trance and leave her on top of a counter.

• Later, at least five bank robberies in Milan were carried out by three well-dressed East Indians. Their method was to approach a teller and ask for change for a high-denomination bill, then quickly hypnotize the teller as he reached for the bill and order him to hand over the cash.

THE U.S. ARMY CORPS OF ENGINEERS

tentatively determined that dredging a channel underneath the northern area of the Great Salt Lake in Utah to develop mineral-extraction ponds would not harm the environment, despite comments on the environmental impact of the operation by one woman, who warned that the action would threaten the "hundreds of peaceful people" living in a submarine city under the lake. The writer said that the village was built by a "de Rothschild" family in pioneer times and then moved beneath the lake to escape Nazis and anti-Semites as well as the "radioactive contaminated environment." The letter considered the Corps' plan as part of "the conspiracy against family de Rothschild."

IMELDA MARCOS SAID THAT NUMEROUS

natural disasters, including Hurricane Andrew, were caused by the restless spirit of her deceased husband, Ferdinand. Seeking permission to bury his body in the Phillipines, Imelda said, "Look at these typhoons, volcanic eruptions, and now what is happening in America. For the sake of the Republic of the Phillipines, for the Filipino people, [we must] put the remains of the president to rest so that these negative vibrations will leave us."

A TEXAS JURY FOUND JANUICE BROWN

guilty of the shooting death of her husband, despite her claims that she killed him to prevent aliens from torturing him forever.

BOB HAIFLEY, OF COVINA, CALIFORNIA,

built a life-size figure of Jesus Christ out of toothpicks, explaining that God had told him to do so. The project consumed 2,500 hours of labor and 65,000 toothpicks of the square, round, flat, and sandwich varieties. Haifley said that God came to him with the project while he was sitting in his truck. He completed the lifelike work, titled "The Gift," despite nerve damage in his left hand and no formal art training. He attributed the project to the belief that God "wants to inspire people."

REYNALDO GONZALES, 33, HIJACKED A

Greyhound bus with eight passengers on board and drove it 320 miles across the desert from Phoenix to Colton, California, before he was shot to death by pursuing police. At the start of his trip, Gonzales had said that Jesus wanted him to leave Arizona for California and that "the devil was chasing up close behind him."

WHEN A SOUTH SEATTLE MAN SHOWED

up at his former place of employment carrying an assault rifle and wearing a bandoleer of ammo across his chest to inquire about back wages, he was assured that he would be given a check. He said that they could mail it and that he was merely on his way to a firing range. Picked up later by the police, the man said that he had a legal right to kill communists and that President Bush "would be next." He also said that he received messages from outer space through tattoos on his arms that were placed there by the Central Intelligence Agency. A search of his home found assault rifles, a shotgun, about 30 boxes, each containing thousands of rounds of ammunition, a pistol, and machetes.

DANIEL HENDRICKS, 34, OF ST. LOUIS,

rammed at least six cars, ran numerous motorists off the road, and overturned a van along a Florida interstate highway before police arrested him when he exited and stopped for a red light. Hendricks told police that he was trying to reach Clearwater so that he could tell the visiting Barbara Bush that Saddam Hussein was going to invade the United States.

A FEDERAL MAGISTRATE ORDERED

Claude L. Philibert, a west Georgia chicken farmer, held for psychiatric evaluation after he dumped the sawed-off head of his pet horse on the steps of the federal courthouse in Atlanta. He took the head from the trunk of his car, which he had driven up the courthouse steps. He said that he took this action to protest a lawsuit he believed an ex-wife had filed against him, although no such suit existed. One of his ex-wives told police that he believed the FBI, CIA, IRS, Nazis, General Electric, and the Mayflower moving company were "out to get him." She also related that he claimed to have visited the Connecticut offices of GE and Mayflower and handed security guards there military helmets with bullets in them, telling the guards that "the people inside will know what this is." He also claimed to have established a "new identity and a Russian name."

IN THE EARLY 1980S, SALLY FOX

of New Orleans began writing to high government officials and the news media, warning that comedian Bob Hope was "violently insane" and possessed the ability to project his thoughts into the minds of others, interfering with the "normal thinking" of Americans. Fox said that she began to "see" Bob Hope whenever she closed her eyes and concentrated. She claimed that a letter to the FBI generated a response in which they told her "they had been getting 800 to 900 complaints a day from people saying the same thing." Fox explained that Hope was too close to Reagan and Bush for them to do anything about her claims and continued writing to members of Congress to urge them to "stop this heinous and vile mental abuse by Bob Hope." Her efforts were apparently reenergized after receiving a letter in August 1991, from a woman in Bergen, New York, who complained of similar "thought disturbances."

HOUSES OF THE HOLY

• In 1973, Timothy Dundon of Altadena, California, began creating a "living monument" in his yard that he claimed would save the human race from destruction. By 1990, the monument, consisting of cattle and horse excrement, had reached a height of 30 feet. "It's awful," said a neighbor. "Especially in the summer. There's flies, flies, flies."

• In front of Japan's Zenshoji Temple sits a statue of Gorufu Kannon, the "Golf Goddess of Mercy," pictured holding a golf ball and putter. Erected by temple priest Shoko Oomi to protect worshipers from stray balls from nearby golf courses, it generated a different response. Golfers now come to worship, offering the goddess balls and tees in hopes of her assisting their games. Said Oomi, "Instead of bowing and praying, they practice swings" before the statue.

• Neighborhood complaints and the local health department cracked down on the religious rituals Donald Moren carried out in his backyard in Lincoln, Nebraska. Moren said that he was told that the burning of chickens, turkeys, and wood atop his "Throne of God," a large altar topped by life-size human figures painted gold, violated the city's health code. "That's life," said Moren. "It's kind of a bother when you are trying to learn and someone stops your offering, but it's nothing you can't live with."

• Police in Coventry, Rhode Island, arrested William R. Silva, 22, after finding that his basement room in the house where he lived with his parents contained an altar and thousands of dollars worth of religious articles stolen from Catholic churches. Priests from the area arrived to inspect candles, linens, church kneelers, statues, a tabernacle, and chalices. In the room, which Silva had labeled "chapel," police also discovered a photo album filled with photographs of the altar decorated for various religious holidays and of Silva standing at the altar dressed in vestments and seemingly performing a mass.

• In July 1990, six followers of David Bawden of Belvue, Kansas, voted to elect him Pope Michael I, head of what they claim is the "true worldwide Catholic Church." "I'm extremely happy that the mystical body has its head back —that the church again has a pope," said Kennett Bawden, David's dad, who described himself as "the pope's father." The group believes that the Catholic Church stopped being the true church with the onset of the Vatican II reforms. Pope Michael, who lives in the basement of his parents' house, runs the church out of a former used-furniture store. Bawden, who gives interviews dressed in clerical garb and

sitting in an orange-velvet cushioned chair, says that he
hasn't yet been ordained and is waiting for one of the remaining "true Catholic" bishops to perform the ceremony.
Asked who those bishops were, he said that he wasn't sure
but that he thought they were "behind the Iron and Bamboo
curtains," cut off from the world and unaware of Vatican II.

WHO ARE THE BRAIN POLICE?

Babel, the Iraqi newspaper published by Saddam Hussein's
son Uday, claimed that during the Persian Gulf War the
United States and Israel used psychic warfare to try to kill
Saddam. "The CIA used psychotronics and biocommunica-
tion to cause a blood clot in the brain or heart of [Saddam],
a procedure that would have obliterated any evidence of the
crime." According to the article, reportedly written by two
Jordanians, the United States and Israel also tried to give
Saddam skin cancer by concentrating cosmic rays on his
skin.

LATE IN 1992, A NUMBER OF REPORTS CIR-
culated among chemical and biological warfare experts that
for more than a year the Yugoslav air force had been dropping mysterious cobwebs onto the territory of Croatia. Cro-
atian scientists reported that there was some evidence that
"the material had induced chromosomal aberrations." Ben-
jamin C. Garrett, director of the Chemical & Biological
Arms Control Institute, examined some of the webs and
said that they consisted of two types of fibers, one of poly-
urethane and one of a protein nature. The material had been
videotaped being dropped from planes. In response to the

accusations, the Yugoslav air force at first claimed that the webs were part of an antiaircraft defense and then denied any drop of any webs whatsoever. Garrett said that the samples did not appear to contain chemical agents or viruses and that he suspected they were part of a "testing of a dissemination agent for biological weapons."

(During World War II, Nazi Germany tested spreading anthrax with silk-thread webs. The U.S. Army reportedly experimented in the 1960s with using spiderwebs as a cheaper method of testing biological agents rather than through aerosol testing.)

NOW THAT'S STRANGE

• A woman on a camping trip in southeastern Australia was struck by lightning as she lay reading the Stephen King novel *The Dead Zone*. Brad Roberts said that he saw the bolt hit his wife Jennifer, 23, on her wristband and then watched as it burned down to her toes. Despite an hour of paralysis, she was hospitalized in good condition. The paperback edition of the novel, which was mostly burned, featured a picture of a man being struck by lightning on its cover.

• Stacey Olson, 17, collapsed and died of heart failure while in gym class at Liberty High School in Spangle, Washington. Two and a half years earlier, his twin brother, Tracey, collapsed and died 50 feet from the spot where Stacey lay.

• Acting on a premonition, Bridgette Simmons, 32, ran four blocks from her job to her home in Tacoma, Washington, to find it ablaze and her husband and son overcome by smoke. She dragged both to safety.

• Four people were killed and one injured when a freak wind

gust hit a car on a rain-slick highway near Bristol, England, on the night of Friday, March 13, 1992. The car was apparently lifted six feet and hurled into a bridge, landing upside down. The car bore the members of the rock band Violent Storm.

SISTER JOSEPHINE CONTRIS, 71, A MEM-

ber of the order of the Sisters of St. Joseph, won $1 million in the California Lottery's Big Spin game. In the game's first level, Sister Josephine picked two numbers, giving her a choice between accepting $40,000 or taking a chance to win more by spinning a wheel. She gave all the winnings to her order. "The sisters always tell me I'm always lucky, so they told me, 'Go for it. Don't just take the $40,000. Go for the million dollars,'" she said.

IN CALIFORNIA IN 1986, U.S. DISTRICT

Court Judge Samuel King, reacting to jurors being absent from court due to heavy rains, declared, "I hereby order that it cease raining by Tuesday." Five years of severe drought followed his ruling.

In February 1991, King announced, "I hereby rescind my order of February 18, 1986, and order that rain shall fall in California beginning February 27, 1991." Later that day, California saw its heaviest rains in a decade. King said that the weather was "proof positive that we are a nation governed by laws."

EVERY JULY 29, THE RESIDENTS OF

Waynesburg, Pennsylvania, gather to pray for rain. On Rain Day 1992 the rain began falling just after 7 P.M., the

98th time in the past 116 years that it rained on Rain Day. According to the town history, a 19th-century farmer made public his findings that it rained on almost every July 29th.

A SOLDIER STATIONED IN THE NORTHERN

China village of Xian, a drought-ravaged area, reported that peasants began performing a rain dance on March 6, 1992, with more than 400 dancing, carrying banners and flags, beating drums, and igniting firecrackers. The soldier said that when rain fell soon after the ceremony, local sorceresses demanded money for the success.

IN 1992, THE PARIS REVIEW FEATURED IN-

terviews with long-dead writers Alice B. Toklas, Gertrude Stein, Henry James, and others. The interviews were conducted via Ouija board.

THE DALAI LAMA ANNOUNCED THAT

Buddhist investigations indicated that his longtime enemy, China's Mao Tse-tung, had been reincarnated as a Chinese boy. "According to some mysterious investigations, usually when somebody has passed away, we start to investigate where they'll be reborn," he said. "According to some indications, Chairman Mao may be reborn three times among the Chinese. Three times."

THE FACE IN THE SPAGHETTI AD

Andrea Johnson, a "certified reverse speech analyst" associated with the Reverse Speech Institute, said that when played backwards, a tape of then-Governor Bill Clinton speaking on CNN's "Larry King Live" in 1992 revealed Clinton's comment, ". . . as you've pointed out, my obituary's been written eight times this year," translated as "All is lost." Johnson termed the discovery a "Stage 3 reversal—the kind that knock your earphones off!" Johnson also claimed that another Clinton comment, on the same show, when played backwards says "Seek marijuana."

IN A COMPLAINT FILED WITH THE FEDERAL

Election Commission, Joseph West of Oakland, California, charged that President George Bush "and/or his agents, since at least as early as November 1991, through the use of satellite technology and computer-generated graphics, did cause subliminal images of George Herbert Walker Bush to be superimposed onto images broadcast on television channels broadcast over cable." West also charged that Bush's face could be found in government photographs and charts, including the food chart pyramid that was designed by the Department of Agriculture, and in a "photograph of the universe (used to explain the big bang theory) by NASA." West went on to say that Bush's face could be detected on the U.S. Postal Service's "Love" stamp and on several USPS postcards.

WOE TO THOSE WITHOUT CABLE

William Tomaszewski, 49, started a support group in New Hope, Pennsylvania, for people who "channel" or communicate with the spirits of the dead. Called Channelers, the group helps novices understand the communication process and teaches them how to communicate with specific dead entities, such as Sammy Davis, Jr., Redd Foxx, and Elvis Presley. Said one 28-year-old man, who turned to the group after he found himself receiving messages from a Commander Zordan from outer space, "I tried telling my friends about it, but they just thought I was crazy. The group helped me to understand that I wasn't the only one with these abilities." Tomaszewski said he was encouraged to start the group by Raphael, an angel channeled by a friend of his.

PROFESSOR CLARE COOPER MARCUS, 58,

a teacher of environmental psychology at the University of California at Berkeley, started a $100-an-hour "house counseling" service in which clients use role-playing to communicate with their homes. The homeowners first speak to their house, letting out all their feelings, then play the role of the house, speaking back to themselves. Said Marcus, "Just as some people keep repeating destructive relationships, some people keep finding themselves in unsuitable houses."

IN MINNESOTA, RAMSEY COUNTY DIS-

trict Judge Joanne Smith ruled against the defense attorney in the rape trial of King Buachee Lee, 28, a Hmong man, who asked that witnesses drink "cursed water" to guarantee their truthful testimony. According to Hmong lore, a person who drinks the substance, a mixture of chicken blood and water, and lies will then face dire consequences, perhaps as severe as death. Judge Smith said that to allow the drinking would have intimidated witnesses and possibly been a health hazard.

LET THE ANSWERING MACHINE GET THIS ONE

In fall 1992, NASA turned on new listening equipment to scan for radio waves from outer space. Along with the media attention to the new venture, 10,000 times more powerful than any instruments used in the search before, came a spate of anecdotal stories from scientists about previous mysterious signals picked up over the years. The famous "Wow!" signal was received by the radio telescope at Ohio State University at 10:16 P.M. on August 15, 1977. The signal, the strongest ever picked up by that system, lasted about 60 seconds and gained its name when a researcher reviewing the computer printouts the next morning scribbled "Wow!" on the margin next to the record of microwave signals. Robert Dixon, head of the university's Search for Extraterrestrial Intelligence program, said, "It wasn't a spacecraft; it wasn't an echo from a satellite. [It was] unmistakably of intelligent origin and had all the hallmarks of coming from an intelligent civilization." Since that day, other strong signals from space have been picked up at radio telescopes in Australia and at Harvard University, among others. Dozens of signals have been picked up that fulfill the expected signature of messages from space but have not been confirmed due to their fleeting nature.

DOOMSDAY REVISITED—OR, WILL MUMMERS BE RAPTURED?

Claims by Lee Jang Lim, 46, a South Korean preacher, that the Rapture would occur on October 28, 1992, caught on among many Christians in that country and spread to the South Korean communities in the United States. According to fundamentalist Christian lore, at the Rapture, 144,000 true Christians will be taken off the face of the Earth and seven years of war and chaos will follow, leading to the Last Judgment. The South Korean government, troubled that the failure of the prophecy to come true might prompt mass suicides, dispatched police agents to Los Angeles, New York, Manchuria, Russia, and Australia to gauge the mood of Korean communities there. Prosecutors in Seoul charged Lee with taking about $1 million from followers. They found $26,711 in banknotes and $828,000 in bank checks and bonds in his house, with some of the bonds due to mature in 1995. Lee explained that he would be returning to Earth after the Rapture. Many of the parishioners at his Dami Missionary Church quit their jobs, sold their homes, and turned their assets over to the church. Some South Korean soldiers deserted in preparation for the end, and officials blamed three suicides on fear of the approaching date. The Korean movement reportedly began with a proclamation by American evangelist Percy Correz, who, addressing churches in Korea, said that the Rapture would occur in 1992 and the beginning of heaven on Earth in 2000. Then three South Korean teenagers claimed to receive revelations that the

Rapture was coming on October 28. One report said that a woman aborted a child so that she would be light enough to be lifted during the Rapture, while another said that believers took martial-arts courses to be able to kick away any who would attempt to hold them onto the Earth during the Rapture.

With Lee in jail, the Rev. Chang Man-ho of the Mission for the Coming Days stood in to lead the congregation on October 28. As the stroke of midnight came and passed with nothing happening, Chang said, "Nothing has happened. Sorry. Let's go home."

RABBI A. JAMES RUDIN, WRITING IN HIS

weekly column for the Religious News Service, said that for years he has received letters signed Jesus or God, which predict the coming end of the world. While at first he used to throw them out, he had a change of mind and has now amassed "an extensive collection of doomsday predictions and personal messages from self-appointed divinities." Rudin said that he wondered how the letter writers "handle the deep frustrations that must surely come when the world, with all its flaws and faults, continues to exist."

THE MATADOR ... THE MATADOR ... THE MATADOR

Vance Davis, 27, leader of the mysterious Gulf Breeze Six —six Army intelligence analysts who went AWOL from their West German post in 1990 and surfaced in Gulf Breeze, Florida, warning of a coming Middle East war and the impending return of Jesus Christ in a UFO—surfaced two years later to reveal that the group took its orders from Ouija board spirits, who warned them of the coming Persian Gulf War and suggested they leave the service "because there's going to be some serious things occurring in the next five years." Davis, who warned of coming earthquakes and the destruction of New York City in a gas explosion, said that he now gives seminars on "self-sustaining lifestyles" and is willing to do ads for Parker Brothers, maker of the Ouija board.

HORSEMEN, PARTY OF FOUR!

The San Francisco-based DOOM group, also known as the Society for Secular Armageddonism, was formed in 1990 to promote "awareness of the coming end of the world." Its Hotline of DOOM, (415) 673-DOOM, features chilling notes of social and environmental dangers affecting the planet. In 1992, DOOM awarded its Global Village Idiot Award to Somali General Mohamed Farrah Aidid for his "extraordinary contribution toward a secular apocalypse." DOOM noted that Aidid was "single-handedly blocking food shipments intended for millions of desperate people [in Somalia]. War and famine, the second and third horsemen of the apocalypse, seem to have found an eager emissary in the general."

WHEN CHRISTIAN RADIO STATION KYCR- AM in Golden Valley, Minnesota, went off the air for two days to repair equipment damaged by a lightning strike, it received many calls from frightened listeners who took the radio silence to mean that either the "government had out-

lawed Christian broadcasting," or that the Rapture had occurred and they had not been lifted up to heaven.

DR. GRAZIELLA MAGHERINI, CHIEF OF

psychiatry at the Santa Maria Nuova Hospital in Florence,
Italy, coined the term "The Stendhal Syndrome," to describe the numerous cases she has treated in more than 10
years of observing tourists who have become disoriented in
the presence of great works of art in that city. Magherini
has collected more than 100 cases in the past decade of tourists who, while visiting the churches and museums of Florence, experience rapid heartbeats, stomach pains, fainting,
heavy perspiration, depression, euphoria, feelings of omnip-
otence, and hallucinations. Although some of those affected
were in the presence of religious paintings (one woman was
convinced that she could hear angels singing), Magherini
said that it is the emotional texture of the artwork that
triggers the reactions along with the factor of the subjects
traveling in a foreign city. Although subjects recover after
a few days of rest, she suggested that tourists not try to
appreciate too much great art in too short a time frame.
Those who seem most susceptible to the phenomena tend to
be single men and women ages 26 to 40 who travel alone or
in small groups and who do not travel often.

MOSHE BEN-MEIR, DIRECTOR OF THE

dead-letter office in Jerusalem, regularly receives letters
from around the world addressed to God as well as to Jesus,
Mohammed, Moses, Solomon, and King David. Ben-Meir
says that when post offices around the world receive such
letters they often forward them to Jerusalem. "Other post
offices assume that God is here—and that I know where to

find him," he said. Some letters bear specific addresses such as "Seventh Heaven, Seat of Honor" or "120 Good Day Street, Garden of Heaven."

WHY NOT THE BEST?

Cambodia's Prince Norodom Sihanouk had to appear on television in 1992 to publicly deny reports sweeping the country that he had made a pact with the devil in which he had been granted more years of life in exchange for the lives of 5,000 Cambodian children under the age of 16. As the hysteria surrounding the story mounted, thousands of children began to wear white threads around their wrists for protection from the devil.

(When Sihanouk was toppled from power in 1970 by Lon Nol, a group of villagers loyal to Sihanouk attacked Lon's brother, Lon Nil, ripping out his liver and then proceeding to a local eatery, where they grilled and ate it.)

BEGINNING IN 1990, THE BELIEF SPREAD

among Argentines that their president, Carlos Menem, was cursed. People pointed to the fact that after he shook the hand of a raceboat driver, the driver proceeded to lose the arm in a crash. Also, Menem appeared on the field with the Argentine soccer team one day before the heavily favored team was defeated 1–0 by Cameroon. Added to this was the fact that several Menem cabinet ministers died while in office. Menem, who consults fortune-tellers, was reported to be very concerned about the growing belief that he was living under a hex.

REGINA LISKA, KNOWN AS REGINA 11,

a self-professed witch, was one of 12 Colombian candidates for the presidency in 1990, having received 74,000 votes in 1986 to qualify as a serious candidate, eligible for free radio and television time with which to campaign. During the race, which she lost, she was the only candidate to regularly predict coming worldwide earthquakes, plagues, and a nuclear accident in Brazil.

THERE IS WIDESPREAD BELIEF AMONG

the people of the Dominican Republic that the name Christopher Columbus is a jinx. When Columbus's name is spoken, one shouts "Zafa" and thrusts forward the little and index fingers of both hands or knocks on wood three times to ward off the curse. The most fervent supporters of the curse theory include the country's political and journalistic elite. Recently, a Dominican newspaper editor compiled the following incidents:

• On August 4, 1946, the 450th anniversary of the founding of the city of Santo Domingo, where Columbus's ashes were buried, the urn containing them was opened. A devastating earthquake struck, obliterating two towns.

• Three planes taking part in a fund-raising drive to build a great lighthouse in honor of Columbus crashed in Colombia, killing the pilots. The planes were named the *Nina*, the *Pinta*, and the *Santa Maria*.

• At the 1948 ceremony inaugurating the beginning of construction of the lighthouse, a dynamite charge sent a boulder down a hill where it crushed the car of the presiding official.

• According to Octavio Amiama, head of the Central Bank's coin museum, an official being awarded the Order of Columbus in the 1940s was pricked by the medal's pin and shortly thereafter died of the ensuing infection.

• Soon after receiving the Columbus medal in 1970, Germany's ambassador, Count Karl von Spreti, was kidnapped and executed by guerrillas.

• Fernando Benitez, Mexican ambassador to Dominica, while writing a book critical of Columbus, experienced broken ribs and a broken hip during the project. "I don't believe in the curse," he said. "But look at all that has happened to me."

(In October 1992, in a ceremony marking the 500th anniversary of Columbus's discovery, the urn bearing his ashes was finally moved to the completed lighthouse.)

WHEN SPANISH SHIPS RECREATING COL-umbus's voyage to the Americas landed in Puerto Rico, 22 crew members jumped ship. They charged the captain with "intimidation" and "mismanagement," blaming him for two collisions at sea, one of which resulted in the *Pinta* taking on 1,000 gallons of water. The malcontents were fired, but then apologized and asked to be rehired, explaining that jobs on historic vessels are scarce.

GUARDIAN ANGELS RISING

In 1991 Pope John Paul II declared that Guardian Angels exist and that they are at work to "help us reach holiness in life." According to a 1990 Gallup Poll, 13 percent of those questioned said that they have had an experience with an angel or devil. Three-quarters of the teenage respondents said that they believed in the existence of angels and half of all Americans agreed.

As of 1992 books and seminars devoted to peoples' encounters with angels were very popular in the United States. The all-angel store Angels for All Seasons opened in Denver, five mail-order companies specializing only in angel-related products opened, including Everything Angels in New York, and the *AngelWatch* newsletter started in New Jersey. Other announced projects included a book on how to communicate with angels, an "angel-a-week" diary, angel calendars, and postcard books. Washington writer Sophy Burnham, author of *Book of Angels*, which appeared in 1990 and is being turned into a Broadway musical, said, "Our angels are brought to us by the yearning of the heart. . . . You have a longing, a deep longing, and that's what attracts the angels to bring the help you need."

WHAT WAS THAT?

• Police, firefighters, and ambulance crews in East Stroudsburg, Pennsylvania, responded to reports that an airplane had crashed in the woods at the end of Normal Street. Witnesses said that they saw flames, smelled smoke, and heard the crash. Yet, a ground and air search found nothing, and no local airports reported any missing aircraft. Stan Gordan, director of the Pennsylvania Association for the Study of the Unexplained, said that during that period there had been several reports of fireballs across the state and that witnesses sometimes reported them as planes crashing.

• A fireball visible along a 200-mile area of the Pacific coast of the United States, from Reedsport, Oregon, to Cape Mendocino, California, created a sonic boom and seemed to trail sparks. It was seen from ships at sea and by witnesses at least 125 miles inland. Authorities speculated that it was a meteorite traveling at 40 times the speed of sound. One observer described it as bright white and then changing colors to yellow and red.

• During the middle of the night of August 21, 1992, powerful tremors rocked Frisian Province in the northern section of the Netherlands, sending hundreds running from their homes, swaying houses, and causing minor damage associated with earthquakes. However, seismic equipment said that the tremors were caused by sound waves from some sort of explosion above or below the ground. Said Hein Haak, director of the seismology department at the Royal Netherlands Meteorological Institute, "We are quite puzzled. We checked all the hypotheses we could think of and none work out." Haak ruled out an underwater explosion, sonic boom, military tests, and tectonic-plate activity, and said that a meteorite hypothesis was the only remaining plausible explanation while admitting at the same time that the data picked up by ground stations did not suggest a meteoric trajectory and more important that no debris had been found. Some witnesses said that they saw a yellowish-red fireball in the sky that night.

• Other mysterious rumblings have shaken parts of California over the last few years. In April 1992, residents of San Gabriel Valley reported an earthquake one morning only to be told that the instruments of the U.S. Geological Survey in Pasadena didn't register an earthquake. A seismologist attributed the shaking to a sonic boom. A similar phenomenon was recorded four times earlier that year between Los Angeles and Sacramento, always at 7 A.M. on a Thursday. *Jane's Defense Weekly*, the London-based military publisher, suggested that those rumblings are due to flights by a new U.S. top-secret spy plane, which they called Aurora (other reporters have said that the plane's name is itself secret), and which reportedly flies at 4,000 mph. Numerous reports over the last few years of strangely shaped aircraft maneuvering near desert bases in California, causing loud sonic booms and leaving a strange "doughnuts-on-a-rope" vapor trail in the sky have all been attributed to the supposed secret craft. The Air Force has repeatedly denied its existence.

• A mystery boom that rocked Ilminster in Somerset, England, on July 29, 1992, had witnesses reporting a howling sound and the "doughnuts-on-a-rope" phenomenon in the sky. *Jane's* attributed that incident to Aurora. Similar booms accompanied by the howling sound and the vapor trail were also reported in Herefordshire and Scotland around the same time.

• In July 1992, London's *Sunday Telegraph* reported that "a mysterious, fast-moving shape in the sky has been scaring sheep in the Mull of Kintyre [Scotland] and rattling windows in Los Angeles."

WHAT'S THAT HUM?

• Since early 1992, the city of Hueytown, Alabama, has been experiencing a loud hum that appears and disappears erratically, sometimes lasting as long as three days only to disappear and start up hours, days, or even a week later. High school math teacher Savina Bradberry described it as "the hum of a fluorescent light tube about to go." The hum keeps some people awake and makes dogs howl. The low-pitched, steady sound, dubbed the "Hueytown Hum," seems to affect mostly one area of 500 homes. Although theories range from electromagnetic forces to high-voltage power lines to huge ventilation fans installed in nearby coal mines, no one has found an explanation. Engineers from USX Corporation, owner of the mines, said that the fans were not causing the sound. The hum is said to be louder on Monday and Tuesday nights and extremely loud on cloudy and rainy days. Mayor Lillian Howard said that "sometimes it comes from the ground and sometimes it vibrates through the air, hitting gutters and walls."

• People in Taos, New Mexico, also have reported a mysterious hum since that summer. Many of those hearing it suffer headaches, loss of balance, irritability, and sleeplessness. Dana Hougland, an acoustical engineer from Denver, measured the sound in a range from 17 hertz (around where human hearing starts) to 70 hertz. "The frequency is low enough that more people tend to feel it rather than hear it," Hougland said. She suggested that it may only be audible to those with acute hearing. In Taos the phenomenon is called "The Sound," and has had similar stress effects on the populace as the "Hueytown Hum." Like Hueytown, the noise sometimes disappears for hours or days only to return unexpectedly. Sometimes witnesses say it is strong enough to rattle windows. Although theories again abound, no one has pinpointed the source of "The Sound."

• After years of complaints from its citizens and lobbying by the Low Frequency Noise Sufferers Association, the British Department of the Environment agreed to investigate claims that many people are hearing a mysterious hum whose source is outside one's head. The department said it would fund research into the phenomenon by the Building Research Establishment near Watford. The research program will study 25 sufferers. And the department acknowledged that about 500 new cases of a low-frequency hum being heard are reported each year.

MYSTERIOUS SMOKE RISING FROM A DRY

river bed in Diyatalawa, Sri Lanka, produced the highest ground temperature ever recorded in that country. Geologists reportedly were as baffled by the 300-degree temperature, which caused plants in the vicinity to wither. Volcanic activity was ruled out as an explanation because Sri Lanka is located outside of any volcanic zone.

DURING SEVERAL WEEKS IN LATE 1992,

200 residents living within a 100-mile radius of Chicago complained to the Federal Aviation Administration that "a black, tarry substance with a greenish tinge" had fallen out of the heavens and onto their property. The victims blamed the frozen human waste known as "blue ice," which is created onboard airplanes. "We cannot demonstrate a link between the dropping and any specific planes," said an FAA spokesman, calling the Chicago area reports "a puzzlement." Chief Tad Leach of the Lincolnwood Police Department said that lab tests on many samples of the droppings allowed him to conclude that "it is from people."

BLESSED VIRGIN MARY WORLD TOUR 1991–1992

• Four women in Patras, Greece, reported sighting the images of Mary and Jesus on a tollbooth at 10 P.M. on September 16, 1991. By midnight that night, a crowd of 2,000 had gathered around the tollbooth.

• For at least two weeks in November 1991, about a dozen women in Santa Ana, California, witnessed a glowing ap-

parition of Mary on tiny blue mosaic tiles at Our Lady of the
Pillar Roman Catholic Church. The women said that the apparition appeared every morning at 7:30, urged them to pray,
and then faded away as they completed the final prayer of a ro-
sary. Some women said that the apparition resembled Our
Lady of the Pillar, while others saw her as Our Lady of Guadalupe. Still others saw her holding the baby Jesus.

• On December 12, 1991, a statuette of Maria de la Rosa
Mistica in a church in Neruquen, Argentina, appeared to
weep bloody tears. The blood was reportedly tested and
found to be fresh blood, but Catholic authorities expressed
skepticism.

• About 6,000 people gathered at the Mother Cabrini Shrine
in Golden, Colorado, on December 8, 1991, awaiting bless-
ings from Mary. Theresa Lopez, 31, of the Denver suburb
of Highlands Ranch, said that Mary had appeared to her as
a crowned woman in October and November and told her
that "great favors shall be rained upon you on my feast day
[December 8]." Sister Bernadette Casciano, administrator of
the shrine, said: "Nothing spectacular or supernatural has
been reported." Lopez, a former manager of a Wendy's,
claimed to have first encountered Mary at Medjugorje in
Yugoslavia. Medjugorje became a popular pilgrimage spot
for Catholics worldwide after six children reported a series
of encounters there with Mary beginning in 1980. Lopez did
claim an encounter on December 8, marking the eleventh
time that Mary appeared to her. Others who claimed to see
a vision by looking into the sun seriously damaged their
eyes. Dr. Lawrence A. Winograd, a Denver ophthalmologist,
treated three people for retina burns. "I'm sure all three
had partial damage of a permanent nature," he said, explaining that the "pretty colors" seen by those staring into the
sun for extended periods are "the exploding cells in the retina sending their last message."

After the December 8 gathering, thousands continued to flock to the shrine, prompting Denver archbishop J. Francis Stafford to order Catholics to stop meeting there. He also initiated an investigation of Lopez's claims. A year later, Marian devotees from around the world were still flocking to the shrine by the busload. In early December 1992, 9,000 Marian followers from 47 states and 10 countries gathered in Denver to attend the three-day Rocky Mountain Marian Conference.

• In late December 1991, hundreds flocked to St. Mary's Roman Catholic Church in Ware, Massachusetts, to see a figure of Mary in a nativity scene that was rumored to have shed tears back in 1989. A priest said that many out-of-towners learned of the earlier event only after a reporter from a Springfield, Massachusetts, newspaper wrote a story about it in 1991.

• Beginning in early February 1992, witnesses said that Mary had appeared on the water tank atop Medalla Milagrosa, a small church in Mar del Plata, Argentina. They said that the image gave off light after sunset.

• Later, in mid-1992, Mary's image was reported on a first-floor classroom window at Nuestra Señora de Lourdes School in La Plata. Witnesses including students, parents, teachers, and priests said that the image remained even after the window was cleaned.

• A janitor at the Shrine of St. Jude in Barberton, Ohio, said that on March 10, 1992, he was confronted by a mysterious woman claiming to be Mary. In the days that followed, other witnesses said that an icon of Mary began to shed tears and that the shrine had been filled with an overwhelming scent of roses, a phenomenon well known at Medjugorje. The janitor said that the woman who appeared to him was around "18, 19, 20," that she had "a glow," and that she talked to him about world government and predicted an attack

against Israel from the north. She told him: "My son's heart
is broken."

• An image believed to be that of Mary appeared in the bedroom mirror of Patricia Galaz in Las Cruces, New Mexico,
around March 6, 1992. Some sort of image was visible in an
AP Wirephoto taken of the mirror two weeks later.

• By March 10, 1992, reports that the Rev. James Bruse, 36,
associate pastor at St. Elizabeth Ann Seton Church in Lake
Ridge, Virginia, had developed the stigmata [wounds to his
hands, feet, and side that resemble those Christ suffered at
his crucifixion] quickly spread nationwide. Church statues
also reportedly wept when Bruse handled them. Hundreds
of people who flocked to the church within days of the dis-
closure reported that a statue of the Virgin Mary wept during a mass celebrated by Bruse. A psychiatrist and a
physician examining the wounds reportedly found no medical or psychological explanations for them.

• About 7,500 people gathered at St. Joseph Roman Catholic
Church in Cold Spring, Kentucky, on the night of August
31, 1992, after the Rev. Leroy Smith, the parish priest, said
that an Ohio mystic told him that his church would be visited by Mary on that date. Despite church statements that
nothing happened that night, many in attendance said that
they did see Mary's image flash in church walls and in a
pine tree and in lights in the sky.

• In the summer of 1992, New Jersey draftsman Joseph Januszkiewicz, 54, revealed that Mary had been appearing to
him for 18 months (since he made a trip to Medjugorje in
1989) and told him that from that point on she would appear
to him only on the first Sunday of each month. Word spread
rapidly, and by the first Sunday in August at least 7,000
thronged to his Marlboro home in hopes of seeing Mary.
Januszkiewicz prayed openly in his backyard before a statue
of Mary, seeming to speak to someone invisible. He later

claimed that he spoke to her and to St. Joseph although none of the thousands claimed to see anything.

About 6,000 showed up in the pouring rain on the first Sunday of September despite advice from the Bishop of the Diocese of Trenton to stay away while the church investigated the sightings. The mayor of the township said that it cost the township $21,000 to provide police protection for the August event alone, adding that he would have to seek state aid for future gatherings. Later in September Januszkiewicz was ordered by the health department to install outside toilets for the thousands expected at the next first Sunday appearance of Mary. By late October Januszkiewicz had joined the Diocese and local police in asking people to stay away from the next expected sighting date. At least 2,000 ignored his wishes and showed up anyway.

• After an elderly woman praying in a shaded grove at Pinto Lake County Park in Watsonville, California, found what she believed was the outline of the Virgin of Guadalupe in the bark of an oak limb above her head, as many as 4,000 people a day began flocking to the site. Park officials had to cordon off part of the tree because pilgrims were carving it up to take bark home as souvenirs.

• In Milford, Connecticut, Claudia Voight reported discovering the face of Jesus Christ in an 80-foot-tall maple tree at the spot where a limb came off during a hurricane in 1985. "It took my breath away," she said. "I told my friend to come over and pretty soon we had the entire neighborhood here."

• By January 1993, as many as 20,000 people were gathering on the 13th of every month at a cow pasture in Conyers, Georgia, to see visions of Mary and Jesus. Event organizer Nancy Fowler said that Mary had appeared to her there five years earlier.

Our Strange Culture

CIVILIZATION, HO!

When a prominent British circus selected California clown Danise "Baby D" Payne to be the star of its Christmas show, British clowns protested by descending on Heathrow Airport on the day of Payne's arrival, throwing custard pies, tickling police officers, and waving placards. "We are funny," said Mr. Jam, a British clown. "American clowns are all shout and glitter."

IN A COURTROOM IN DORTMUND, GER-

many, "The Best Elvis in the Whole World" sued "Germany's Best Elvis" over rights to the claim of the best Elvis impersonator in Germany. The judge decided in favor of "The Best Elvis in the Whole World" and admonished both about future unclear advertisements.

WILLIAM MORROW PUBLISHERS PAID LIO-

nel Dahmer $150,000 to write a book titled *My Son*, about the raising of his son, serial killer Jeffrey Dahmer. "At the very least, it would be useful to fathers and mothers everywhere to learn from my experience," Dahmer explained in his book proposal. He added that his interactions with his son consisted of "mostly short periods of quality time."

A TELEVISION COMMERCIAL IN TAIWAN

promoting Church's Fried Chicken compared the product's greatness to a Roman leader, a Chinese emperor, and Adolf Hitler. While one actor eats the chicken, another dressed as Hitler salutes the camera.

MICHAEL MOORE, 24, AUTHOR OF THE

book *Cheating 101: The Benefits and Fundamentals of Earning the Easy "A,"* said that he learned many cheating secrets from students at the University of Maryland, the University of Virginia, and Mount St. Mary's College. Moore explained that the purposes of the book are to "teach kids how to cheat and to let people know what's going on, to let them in on college's dirty secret." Among the techniques listed are entering notes on a pocket calculator and on calculator watches, scribbling data in code on your desk the night before, and arranging to have yourself paged out of class by a beeper in order to call a student standing by with your notes. Asked how he could ethically write such a

book, Moore replied, "Ethically? I think that's just a term that's tossed around. I don't think there's too many ethics around. I don't think too many people have ethics anymore."

HOPING TO STOP WIDESPREAD CHEATING

on school exams, Bangladesh imposed a new law prescribing that children as young as 14 who are caught cheating on finals can be jailed for up to 10 years. Teachers found leaking test questions or tampering with scores risk the same fate.

LINDA AND DAVID DUNLAP PRODUCED

a video, "The Fine Art of Dumpster Diving," which uses a talk-show format to warn homeless people about the dangers of eating from trash bins and provide tips on how to avoid food poisoning from discarded food tainted by chemicals, rodents, and germs. "All we are trying to do is to help the homeless survive a little less painfully," said Linda.

WE CONTROL THE HORIZONTAL

• *Pravda* reported in 1991 that during the 10 previous years 2,134 people had been killed and scores injured when Soviet-made television sets exploded. The explosions were attributed to defective parts.
• Some 7,000 Britons a year are hospitalized as a result of watching television, according to the government survey. Some people faint during gory scenes, whereas others are injured while attempting to do chores and watch TV at the same time. Noteworthy mishaps included a man who hurt

his hand punching the screen during a boxing match and a rugby fan who jumped for joy when his team scored and crashed into a chandelier.

• After reports that 10 television sets had exploded or caught fire in five months, the Dutch consumer safety institute established a consumer hot line. More than 200 people called in its first week to report that their televisions had experienced the same problems. The institute said that the explosions and fires were experienced by a variety of brands. One fire official suggested that remote controls might somehow be at fault.

AFTER AN EPISODE OF THE "G.I. JOE" SAT-

urday morning cartoon show had G.I. Joe battling evil forces trying to destroy the Earth's ozone layer by siphoning chlorofluorocarbons from giant aerosol tanks of shaving cream, the Consumer Aerosol Products Council launched an education campaign directed at young people to make them aware that aerosols no longer contain CFCs since they were outlawed in 1978.

FLORIDA'S COCONUT CREEK HIGH SCHOOL

refused to send a teacher to Thee Dollhouse III strip club to verify the employment of an 18-year-old senior in order to grant him work-study credit. "They're being very unopen-minded about this," said bar helper Dino Magazzeni. "I mean, this is the '90s." The club employed Magazzeni's mother as the "house mom" for the dancers and his sister as a waitress.

AUTOMOBILITY AGE

The car was convicted of fundamental abuses of human rights at a mock trial at the 1992 annual conference of the Australian and New Zealand Association for the Advancement of Science. The car was implicated in the deaths of 250,000 to 500,000 people daily and the maiming of millions more. It also was accused of systematically destroying public space, robbing children of play areas and cultural activity, discriminating against society's disadvantaged, encouraging social segregation and preventing spontaneous interaction between people. David Engwicht, an urban transport activist who served as prosecutor at the trial, said, "The car must never again be allowed to rule our streets."

• New York City police arrested Albert Simon, 28, for shooting his car after it broke down in traffic. "One man opened the hood and began to tinker," said Transit Police Officer James Hilbert, who had seen the car sputter to a stop. "The other guy pulled out a gun and fired four rounds into the windshield."

• Michael Beeckman was sentenced to three months in jail by a Belgian court for shooting up a car with a submachine gun. Beeckman explained that he shot the car because it had passed his car in traffic.

• A motorist, angry that a woman driver wouldn't let him pass, pulled up and shot her 25-year-old husband, who was sitting in the front passenger seat, hitting him just above his right temple. While in the emergency room at Desert Samaritan Medical Center in Mesa, Arizona, his nose began to bleed. A police officer handed him a towel and he blew the bullet out of his nose. Doctors said the bullet must have lodged in a sinus.

• According to the Utah Highway Patrol, 23-year-old Som-pasong Norphengvadith drove his Datsun 280Z at speeds in excess of 100 miles per hour until he blew his engine and pulled onto a highway median. As police approached, he locked himself in his car and pretended to have a gun under his coat. After a 1½-hour standoff, a SWAT team broke one of the car's windows, then threw tear gas and smoke bombs inside. Norphengvadith threw them back out. The SWAT team threw them back in, and he tossed them out again. Finally, the SWAT team smashed the driver-side window and pulled him out of the car. Norphengvadith had no gun, his car held no illegal substance, and he had no police record. "We still don't understand why he was so uncooperative," said police. "It was totally irrational behavior."

• Police reported a new twist on auto theft: young people ramming police cruisers with stolen cars. Some of the rammers try to pop air bags in their pursuers' cars to slow them down. Others steal two cars, one fancier than the other, lure police into an intersection with the nicer car, then use the "junk car" to ram police. Authorities in New Jersey's Essex and Union counties, which include four of the top 10 cities in per capita car theft, theorize that the rammers are a mix of joyriders with a bad attitude toward police and harder-core thieves who steal cars for profit.

Newark officials announced they were stepping up efforts to stem the city's rash of car thefts by creating a team of 25 specially trained police officers to comb the city for cars reported stolen. Mayor Sharpe James explained that the officers would be armed with non-lethal paint guns and, instead of chasing the stolen vehicles, would shoot blue or yellow fluorescent paint at them. The mayor urged residents to call the police whenever they spot a vehicle with a telltale paint blob.

• The latest twist on car theft in Detroit is stealing air bags.

According to *Car & Driver* magazine, unexploded bags can be fenced to repair shops, which sell them to unsuspecting customers. A standard replacement air bag costs $800, the magazine said, "but crooked shops can buy the stolen ones for as little as $100."

• After discovering that someone had stolen his car in White Hall, Arkansas, Samuel Jones was standing in the parking lot where he worked when a man pulled up beside him and explained that he had gotten lost and needed directions. The man was driving Jones's car. Jones communicated to a nearby security guard that he needed assistance, then gave the man directions until police arrived and arrested him.

• Baltimore police said a suspected car thief was found lying wounded next to a stolen vehicle, apparently having been beaten on the head by a steel anti-theft bar, known as "The Club."

• When a car with two men pulled in front of Anne Stern, 73, as she was driving to a Thanksgiving gathering in Valley Stream, New York, she tried to escape by driving across lawns. According to police, the men chased her and began ramming her car. When she finally stopped, one of the men banged on her window and, when she lowered it to scream, grabbed her. She shifted into reverse and dragged him down the street. When he let go, Stern chased him until he jumped back into the other car, which fled. "I think they were carjacking virgins," Stern said.

• In Venice, Italy, two drivers collided at a railroad crossing. While they left their cars on the tracks and argued over who was at fault, a Milan-bound train came along and smashed into the cars, sending them into the path of another train pulling into Venice. A spokesperson for the Venice station said 20 trains carrying some 20,000 people were held up for two and a half hours while the tracks were cleared of debris.

• Los Angeles police investigating a rash of apparently staged high-speed accidents between cars and tractor-trailers charged more than 20 people with running five freeway crash rings to collect insurance money. Evidence included "wreck scripts" found in the suspects' apartments and glove compartments. Authorities explained that ringleaders and recruits—usually desperately poor Hispanic immigrants paid as little as $100 to ride in crash cars—would pull in front of giant rigs on the city's freeways, then brake suddenly to cause rear-end collisions.

• The National Highway Safety Administration acknowledged receiving complaints of air bags injuring and killing motorists, but said agency policy prevents an investigation. Because the problems have occurred in too many different makes of car, instead of any particular model, they fail to meet the minimum standards for triggering a safety probe.

• In Lanesboro, Minnesota, Lyle Harlos, 37, tried to kill a rat living in his garage by gassing it with carbon monoxide from his car exhaust. Fumes seeped into the house from the attached garage, according to Olmsted County Coroner Paul Belau, and killed Harlos.

• Twice in two days, Sergio Garcia doused a car with gasoline, punctured its tires, and set it ablaze on Chicago's Michigan Avenue Bridge during evening rush hour. Written on the vehicle's hood was the message: "I come in the name of Jesus Christ, my father, to save America." "I love you" was written on the trunk. After he was apprehended watching the second blaze, Garcia said, "I come from the father."

• The 1992 annual "Blessing of the Cars" in Los Angeles occurred as scheduled, but without the actual blessing. The previous year, a priest standing in a drive-through booth blessed an estimated 200 cars. In 1992, the city contributed $5,000 to sponsor an art and custom car show as part of the annual event, so organizers said the religious ceremony it-

self had to be eliminated because it would have violated the
constitutional separation of church and state.

Instead of the blessing, the several thousand people
who attended saw a puppet show, also titled "The Blessing
of the Cars." It featured a 12-foot-high Jesus-like figure in
purple robes swaying back and forth in a gesture of blessing. Also appearing were cardboard pedestrians with tar-
gets on their chests, a block-headed mechanic who
undulated in time to rock music, frenzied drivers in evening
clothes, and a dancing gasoline pump.

• In Contra Costa, California, the Parkhaven Baptist Church
has put on its annual drive-through Passion Play since 1985.
Worshippers witness the sufferings of Jesus Christ from
their own cars. Chip Seay, the church pastor, developed the
drive-by drama and a similar Christmas pageant to illus-
trate the real meaning of holidays to people who might be
reluctant to enter a church. Motorists are given a one-min-
ute audiotape, which directs them through five scenes depicting the Last Supper, Christ's arrest, the trial, the
Crucifixion, and the Resurrection. About 30 parishioners
perform at the event, which Seay said is seen by as many
as 5,000 people a year.

• In Arizona, officials at Phoenix International Raceway
halted the Solar & Electric 500 race when an electric car's
battery leaked a toxic chemical. The driver and 14 other
people were taken to the hospital after breathing fumes.

• Within a year after Albania legalized private cars, they
became a menace in a country where there are few road
signs and no general agreement on whether to drive on the
right or left side of the road. Although Albania has just
40,000 licensed drivers, during the first half of 1992, 166 pedestrians were killed by cars, most of them autos unsafe to
drive.

Many of the 40,000 cars that have appeared on the

crumbling highways since the government approved private ownership are battered, worn-out Mercedes, Fiats, and Volkswagens that arrive by ferry and are sold at the dock in Durres. "Europe is helping Albania with food," Hysni Malko, Albania's chief traffic officer, observed, "while Albania is helping it by taking all the old cars from the graveyards of Europe."

• New York City's Department of Transportation started posting "Walk Alert" decals on signposts at dangerous intersections in an effort to reduce the number of pedestrian deaths (1,388 from 1988 to 1991) and injuries (14,959 in 1991). Among the stickers' advice: "Beware of rear wheels mounting sidewalk" and "Hold your arm up high when crossing. Drivers will be able to see you better."

• Traffic in the Greek capital of Athens was snarled by mice and rats gnawing through traffic-light cables. City officials added that the traffic jams were compounded by maintenance workers, who knocked out many of the signal lights with high-pressure water hoses they were using to wash off accumulated pigeon droppings.

• Twenty percent of German motorists surveyed revealed that they enjoy being stuck in traffic—but only during their leisure time, not on the way to work. Professor Horst W. Opaschowski of the BAT leisure research institute said his poll of 2,482 drivers uncovered a "secret love of traffic snarls. Men in particular have nothing against a bit of chaos on the roads." One driver explained, "I come back from an exhausting jam feeling really good."

JOHN AND FLORENCE BAHMA OF TUC-

son, Arizona, were turned away from the polls on election day because they were wearing green sweaters. Larry Bahill, director of the Pima County Elections board, had issued orders by which to decide what amount of green clothing at a voting site might be subtle campaigning by the state's new Green Party. "I told my people that if just one person came in wearing green, go ahead and let 'em vote," said Bahill. "But, if several people came in wearing green," they were to be instructed that "one of them had to wait outside while the other one cast a vote. And if they weren't willing to do that, they both had to leave." Neither John Bahma, a registered Republican, nor his wife, a registered Democrat, had planned to vote for the Green Party. She was eventually allowed to vote after taking off her sweater.

OFFICIALS OF INDIA'S BOMBAY MUNICIPAL

Corporation oversee 85 "night rat killers" (technically referred to as NRKs) who patrol the city at night beating rats to death with sticks. Each NRK has a quota of 25 rats a night. Most expert NRKs fill their quota within the first two hours of their shift each night, leaving the rest of their hours free for other work, according to one overseer, who added, "I can easily make out a rat beaten to death from a poisoned rat," for which an NRK receives no credit. From April 1, 1991, to March 31, 1992, the 85 NRKs beat to death 369,487 rats. One taxi driver explained that he became an NRK because "I wanted a fixed job that brought a regular salary."

URBAN MINERS

• Police serving a warrant on Eugene Peek found 73 pay phones in his Bronx apartment. The phones had been stolen from the Port Authority and the street. Police said that

Peek, a crack addict, told them that he took the phones because he was hungry.

• Jose Molina was caught with 46 stolen parking meters at his Brooklyn apartment. Each meter, connected to its metal pipe, weighed about 80 pounds. Police theorized that a thief would have to wrap a chain around each and then drag it out of the ground with a car or truck.

CLIENTS WHO CONCEIVE BY IN VITRO FERtilization at Pacific Fertility Centers, based in San Francisco, can get a photo of their two-day-old embryo taken through a microscope. One recipient described her first look at the two- to six-cell embryo as "total magic."

HERE WE ARE, NOW— ENTERTAIN US!!!

Bar owner Eric Doppen's installation of a Breathalyzer at his disco in Groenlo, Netherlands, didn't exactly have the desired effect. Instead of worrying about their fitness to drive, Doppen explained, patrons of the City Centrum disco began "lining up to use it to referee their drinking competitions."

PEOPLE IN ENGLAND BEGAN PAYING TO take part in a make-believe prisoner-of-war getaway weekend. Participants get to dress in wartime uniforms and take part in work parties, roll calls, and escape attempts at an abandoned Royal Air Force base in Hampshire.

FACED WITH A SHORTAGE OF HEROIN AND marijuana, Malaysian drug addicts turned to sniffing fresh cow dung. Users wait for the cow dung and then quickly place a coconut shell over it, inhaling the methane gas through a hole at the top of the shell. "You may find the cow dung smelly and awful," Deputy Interior Minister Megat Junid Ayob said, "but for them it is heaven."

THE SILENT MEETING CLUB IN PHILADEL- phia was founded for people to meet at various randomly chosen locations around that city and sit or stand there together, silently enjoying the scene. The length of meetings is up to each individual member, and the only rule is to remain silent. John Hudak said that he founded the club after observing that "most people you meet feel they're forced to say something, even if they have nothing to say." He added, "Even if someone comes an hour later and there's no one there, it's still a valid part of the meeting."

THE FOREST SERVICE RENOVATED TWO dozen abandoned lookout towers in western national forests and began charging vacationers $30 a night to sleep in them. The towers offer 360-degree views but tend to be sparsely furnished, sway in the wind, and lack plumbing. They also are often struck by lightning.

DRAWBRIDGE DIVING HAS BECOME SO prevalent among young people in the Netherlands that the government had to institute an information campaign warning of its dangers. To play, youngsters stand on the edge of a rising bridge span and then dive into canals below from heights of up to 30 feet. As a variation, some dangle by their fingers from the span's edge as it descends to close, letting go at just the last second to fall into the water below.

EVERYTHING YOU KNOW IS WRONG

• According to a German public opinion poll, reported by *Der Spiegel* in 1992, 27 percent of those questioned said that if Hitler hadn't massacred Jews and started the war he would have been a great statesman. Forty-two percent said that the Nazis had their good sides.

• *Glamour* magazine reported that in a survey of 1,045 men, ages 20 to 39, one-third would have their penises enlarged if the operation was "free, quick and painless." Fifty-eight percent of the respondents said that they would choose an intensely erotic kiss over just average sex.

• According to *Child* magazine, researchers at Case Western Reserve University medical school discovered that only 30 percent of boys and 21 percent of girls know the correct names for their genitals. After conducting interviews with mothers of 1- to 4-year-olds, they found that 35 percent of boys and 17 percent of girls are taught no names at all for their genitals.

• Shown a list of recent movies and asked which one they would most like to see turned into a theme park ride, 20 percent of the respondents picked *Lethal Weapon*. Eleven percent selected *The Silence of the Lambs*.

• A study by sociologists Jim Gundlach of Auburn University and Steven Stack of Wayne State University suggested that the themes prevalent in country music "foster a suicidal mood among people already at risk of suicide." (Not long after the study's release, police in Belton, Missouri, shot and killed Joe Baugher, 48, when he barricaded himself in his house and began shooting. Baugher had said that he was angered by a radio station's ban on the music of Hank Williams, Jr.)

THE TOWN OF SALEM, NEW HAMPSHIRE,
gave town manager Barry Brenner a one-year contract extension, but said it was valid only if he cleans up his desk and keeps it clean. Selectman Joseph Gagnon explained that mountains of paper prevented Brenner from letting people into his office, adding that earlier in the year town check vouchers got lost in the pile for six months.

JAPAN'S LABOR MINISTRY ANNOUNCED
plans to set up 347 health centers nationwide to combat the rise of "karoshi," or death from overwork.

THE $270 BILLION DEFENSE BUDGET THAT
the House of Representatives approved in 1992 contained a provision to repeal a five-year-old ban on the military's buying manual typewriters from former Warsaw Pact members.

IN A 1992 BASEBALL GAME BETWEEN ATlanta and Philadelphia, with a runner on first base and one out, Braves pitcher Charlie Leibrandt recorded his 1,000th career strikeout. Catcher Greg Olson threw the ball back to Leibrandt, who rolled it toward the dugout so he could keep it as a memento. Realizing he had forgotten to call time out

first, Leibrandt ran after the ball. He couldn't get it before it went in the dugout, whereupon the runner was awarded second base and Leibrandt was charged with an error.

FOUL MOUTHS

• Shakespearean lecturer Jane Wirgman made an effort to clean up the language of prisoners at England's Norwich Prison by familiarizing inmates with 400-year-old insults popular in Shakespeare's time. Prisoners there reportedly began calling each other "thou crusty botch of nature" and "thou odiferous stench."
• University of Sydney language expert Brian Taylor said that people who move to Australia should be taught swear words so they can adjust to the culture, knowing when they are being insulted and how to appropriately respond. Taylor explained that "virtually everybody swears now" and those unfamiliar with the terms could risk injury.

THE ENGLISH TOURIST BOARD REPORTED

that the fastest-growing tourist attraction was the Sellafield nuclear-fuels reprocessing plant, the largest recycler of nuclear waste in the world. Tourists and students come by the busloads to tour such exhibits as a model of a reactor core. As one walks through, voices on a monitor describe the operations, saying things such as: "Feel the power . . . rods hot with fission . . . all so controlled." The director of tourism noted that "about 90 percent of our visitors are more positive about nuclear power having been through the center."

THE WORLD ESKIMO-INDIAN OLYMPICS,

which date back centuries but whose recent form began as an annual competition in 1960, drew some 500 contestants in 1992 and a hint by the announcer that "we might see some blood." Among the 18 events were the "ear pull"—each of two contestants ties a twine of dried seal gut around one of their ears and then they pull their heads away from each other until one gives up; the "seal hop"—contestants hop across a floor, landing only on their knuckles and toes; the "four man carry"—one person must carry four other men; the "greased pole walk"—contestants have to walk along a 12-foot spruce log that has been coated with Crisco; and "ear weight-lifting"—contestants must lift the weight-equivalent of a bowling ball with their ear and carry it that way for as far as they can. (The record, set in 1984 by Joshua Okpik, Jr., was more than a half mile.)

TRAMPING THE DIRT DOWN TWICE

During 1992 several former world leaders were exhumed and then buried again.

• In Ethiopia, workers found the remains of Emperor Haile Selassie, who died in 1975 at the age of 83, buried under the office floor of former president Mengistu Hasile Mariam, the man who overthrew him. According to state radio, the remains were put there "to see that the body did not rise from the dead." His family announced that it planned to rebury him at the Orthodox cathedral.

• In Ghana, Kwame Nkrumah, the continent's first post-colonial president, was buried with full military honors at a park where he first declared the country's independence from Britain in 1957. He had died in exile in Bucharest in 1972, and his body was first buried in his home village in Ghana.

• Liberia's Prince Johnson, leader of the rebels in that country, put the corpse of former president Samuel Doe on display because Johnson's father was in town for a visit and asked to see it. Johnson tortured Doe to death in 1990, at one point cutting off his ears to let him bleed to death, and videotaped the whole episode. The exhumed body was publicly shown on a slab of zinc.

• In Albania, government workers were ordered to dig up the body of former Communist boss Enver Hoxha from his official burial vault and rebury him in a cemetery for commoners. That same night, the bodies of about a dozen top Communist officials were also exhumed and moved to the more simple surroundings. Hoxha, who died in 1985, is widely reviled by Albanians, who also rejected his party in their first free elections.

DR. SERGEI S. DEBOV, THE MAN IN

charge of preserving Lenin's body for the past 40 years, revealed how it was done. The reason Lenin's body, in display in a glass sarcophagus in Red Square, looked so well preserved is that a secret embalming compound was used to replace all the water in his skin. The body was then kept at 16 degrees Celsius and 70 percent relative humidity. Sensors and monitors controlling these conditions were constantly watched by a staff of 10 specialists. The team gave Lenin a checkup every Monday and Friday for 40 years, daubing embalming fluid on his hands and head. Every 18 months he was given a bath in embalming compound and every five years he was thoroughly inspected by a team of senior scientists.

NEW WORLD ORDERS

In preparation for the third anniversary of the 1989 Tiananmen Square massacre, the Chinese government issued a ban on crying or laughing at a memorial there.

KUWAIT'S CHARITY COMMITTEE FOR THE

Marriage Project urged married men to take more wives (up to the Islamic legal limit of four) in order to deal with the problem of "spinsterhood." Saying there were too many unmarried Kuwaiti women, the charity offered men up to $2,800 in loans, cheap kitchenware, and free furniture.

SANTA CRUZ, CALIFORNIA, INSTITUTED AN

"anti-lookism" statute, prohibiting discrimination against people whose looks might make people discriminate against them—the overweight, the underweight, those tall and short, and others exhibiting extreme physical traits. Local Chamber of Commerce officials, who dubbed the law the "ugly ordinance," said they feared that it would prevent businesses from hiring people who wore outrageous or otherwise inappropriate attire.

A few months later, Philippine congressman Rudolfo Albano responded to complaints from applicants who had been denied government jobs because "they are ugly, short or because they have physical defects," by sponsoring a bill forbidding government agencies from discriminating against job applicants on the basis of "facial features, build and height." The measure would exempt modeling and public relations jobs.

THE GERMAN PARLIAMENT'S COMMIS-

sion on children proposed making it a violation of civil law
for German parents to engage in "spanking, boxing ears,
withholding affection, constant nagging, or threatening children with the bogeyman." A review of other German laws
already in place noted that citizens there are forbidden to
make angry gestures toward other motorists, cannot insult
civil servants, and are forbidden to give a child a name that
is not on a government-approved list of names.

THE GOVERNMENT OF INDIA INTRODUCED

a bill that would ban the transport of Indian children to
Persian Gulf emirates where they are often used as jockeys
in camel races. A government spokesman pointed to 20 recent cases in which Indian diplomats rescued Indian children smuggled to several Gulf states for such purposes.
According to Indian police, young Indian boys are strapped
to camels and their shrieking makes the animals run faster
during races.

THE MALAYSIAN HOME AFFAIRS MINIS-

try ended its ban on long-haired rock groups performing on
television and radio after the lead singers from two groups
agreed to have their hair cut by a government official on
the television program "Good Morning, Malaysia." Information Minister Mohamad Rahmat personally cut the hair
of lead singers Amy of the band Search and Awl of the band
Wings.

UP IN THE MORNING AND
OFF TO SCHOOL

• Reacting to complaints by Candy Johnson, mother of a second-grader at Doctors Inlet (Florida) Elementary School, officials dropped the use of a puppet named Pumsy the Dragon as a teaching tool. Teachers had used the dragon for four years to teach self-esteem and decision-making to first- to third-graders, but Johnson said that the puppet was hypnotic and could threaten a child's welfare. Other critics believed Pumsy to be a tool of New Age and occult ideas.

• In Lansing, Michigan, a model health class stopped teaching students to relieve stress by taking several deep breaths after some parents complained that the technique promoted mysticism. "People will come and testify like mad that it creates out-of-body experiences and undermines Christianity, most of which we just never understood as being a realistic concern," said Don Ben Sweeney, spokesperson for the Michigan Model for Comprehensive Health Education, explaining that the students now would be taught to manage stress by counting to 10 or resting their head on their desk.

• Police in Taylor, Michigan, a Detroit suburb, probed leads suggesting that a group of four teachers in a school welding shop manufactured machine guns, which they then sold for $500 each. Sources said that the teachers may have paid two students to work in the shop after school hours welding parts for the guns.

• The University of Florida's student government began distributing anti-drunken driving pledge cards to about 9,000 students. The cards are good for one free beer when the student signs the pledge on the back promising not to drive drunk. Students are limited to one card a day.

AT THE EUROPEAN FINE ART FAIR IN

Maastricht, Netherlands, where a pencil sketch by Vincent van Gogh sold for $120,500, an ornate 18th-century toilet fetched $205,200.

WHEN A LOS ANGELES CITY AGENCY PRO-

posed allocating $175,000 for three street paintings on Hollywood Boulevard, critics attacked the move as wasteful. They noted that the artworks would fade under the tire treads.

DARRYL MALONE, 29, FILED A COMPLAINT

with the Nevada Equal Employment Opportunity Commission after he was fired when he charged his employer with sexual discrimination for repeatedly passing him over for promotion because he was a man. For eight months, the 165-pound ex-Marine impersonated a woman, named Raven, on a phone-sex line for Northwest Nevada Telco.

BEFORE SENDING TROOPS TO SOMALIA,

the United States announced that it was trying to stop rampant theft of food shipments by sending the Somalis food they don't like. Andrew Natsios, assistant administrator of the Agency for International Development, explained that corn and sorghum being sent are ideal for free food distribution because they are nutritious enough to alleviate hunger but not popular enough to command high black market prices.

DESPITE UNITED NATIONS SANCTIONS
and destruction caused by the Persian Gulf War, the Iraqi government said it hopes to boost tourism by attracting foreigners. Although there are abundant historical sights, getting to Iraq involves a 13-hour drive from Amman, Jordan. What's more, prices in Baghdad are sky-high, according to Reuters, which reported that a hamburger at a hotel costs $70.

THAT VOODOO THAT YOU DO SO WELL

• Despite her claims that she was simply praying over her students, a Bronx public school teacher was suspended for three days for performing "exorcisms" in her classroom. Students said that their teacher was placing her hands on their heads "to drive out the devil."

• Police in Irvington, New Jersey, arrested a substitute teacher for reportedly performing "voodoo" rituals on a class of rowdy seventh-graders and for threatening to burn their houses down. According to Police Director Samuel G. Williams, the teacher "waved the cross at them, took out some kind of powder and threw the powder about the class, and said all their souls were going to go to the Lord." She also told the students that she knew where they lived.

• In Florala, Alabama, former mayor H. T. Mathis, 89, who was impeached in 1988, ran for the office again with a new campaign promise: "No more voodoo." During his term, Mathis accused his police chief of being a witch, sprinkled a mysterious dust around City Hall to get the chief to leave town, and called a midnight news conference to proclaim

National Voodoo Week. "I had some bad advice when I did that," Mathis admitted.

In the September 1992 primary, Mathis finished sixth in a seven-candidate field, receiving just 18 votes. "I don't know how many people told me they were going to vote for me," he said. "There must be something wrong somewhere."

THE U.S. MILITARY AUCTIONED OFF "EX-cess scrap equipment" left behind in Saudi Arabia after Operation Desert Storm for about $16 million, according to the Defense Department. The biggest buyer of the remains of American planes and helicopters, captured Iraqi tanks, and assorted vehicles was Jumaa al-Jumaa, who paid $13.3 million for the scrap material, which contains valuable titanium, as well as brass, zinc, aluminum, and steel. Within a month, al-Jumaa told Reuters that he had already sold a third of his purchases for a hefty profit.

WHEN LANDLORD PER HATLEN WENT TO
the house he had rented to a 44-year-old man and his wife in Vestby, Norway, he found they had gone but left behind more than 1,000 rats. The renter, who was reported to be in hiding, told police he liked rats and wanted to breed them for pet stores, but the situation got out of control.

TWENTY PERCENT OF FRENCH WOMEN,
according to a survey reported in the newsmagazine *Le Point*, do not think an interviewer should be censured for asking a job applicant to disrobe.

MANY WORKERS IN THE CASH-STRAPPED

former Soviet Union are having to settle for payment in kind instead of paychecks. Itar-Tass news agency reported that at the Brest Stocking Factory, where the average pay is about $14 a month, contracts specify that a worker's pay can include 10 pairs of pantyhose and 50 pairs of socks, worth about $10.

RESIDENTS OF THE CENTRAL SPANISH

town of Aranjuez, celebrated in one of the country's best-known classical works, Joaquin Rodrigo's "Concerto de Aranjuez," complained to their mayor that they are fed up with being forced to hear it 48 times a day. A new clock in the Plaza de la Constitucion plays the first 15 seconds of the piece every hour and half-hour. The national Popular Party asked the mayor to ban the music from midnight to 8 A.M. "to protect the citizens' right to get some rest."

BEFORE FILING AS A DEMOCRATIC CAN-

didate for lieutenant governor in Missouri, St. Louis businessman Richard T. Pisani officially changed his name, enabling him to be listed on the ballot as "Richard Thomas Bullet Train Pisani." Pisani explained that he wanted voters to know that he is a booster of a proposed high-speed train across the state.

IN THE MINNESOTA HOUSE OF REPRE-

sentatives, Representative Sidney Pauly held up a bill to designate square dancing as the state dance, even though quick passage had been expected. Noting that she had nothing against square dancing, Pauly explained: "All of a sudden this comes through like greased lightning. I have a serious bill, but can't get a hearing."

Pauly complained that she has campaigned for four years trying to win support for her measure to name a state book. Her choice is Laura Ingalls Wilder's *On the Banks of Plum Creek*, on which the television show "Little House on the Prairie" was based.

INDIA'S CHIEF ELECTION COMMISSIONER,

T. N. Seshan, barred political candidates and their parties from using animals as symbols. He explained that the official action was necessary to stop supporters of rival factions from torturing and killing the actual animals representing their opponents.

WHAT CAN THE CHINESE SCHOOL SYSTEM TEACH US?

• Li Yuan, 21, a student at the college in Zhengzhou, in China's central Hunan province, was already facing expulsion for "long-term indecent relations" with a fellow student when she allegedly mixed 12.3 ounces of white arsenic into a batch of fermented dough at the school cafeteria. She succeeded in poisoning 788 people, all but 11 requiring hospitalization. Li Yuan was described as someone who "hated everything on earth."

• A Chinese court sentenced teacher Liu Deshun, 26, to two years in jail for forcing unruly grade-school students to eat cow dung as punishment on at least 56 occasions. Liu meted out the punishment for talking out of turn, fighting, and handing in homework late. The *Beijing Evening News* noted that the "normal studying process" was affected when students began "vomiting without stopping after they ate the cow dung."

ONE OF PRESIDENT BUSH'S CONTRIBU-

tions to Japanese culture, courtesy of his visit to Tokyo, is the introduction of a socially acceptable verb for the act of vomiting: "Bushusuru." The Baltimore *Sun* reported that the new word quickly found its way into popular magazines, television variety shows, even a trained-monkey act—when the monkey hears the word, it imitates the president throwing up on Prime Minister Kiichi Miyazawa, complete with realistic sounds.

The paper observed that the word has special usefulness in Tokyo, where each night thousands of Japanese men deliberately get drunk as fast as they can to escape "the rigid manners that dominate Tokyo's social relations. As these tens of thousands of men head for the subways around midnight, dozens each night get no farther than the sidewalk before they Bushusuru."

PROTESTING A 1990 VISIT BY VICE PRESI-

dent Dan Quayle to Portland, Oregon, a group of more than 20 artists calling themselves the Reverse Peristalsis Painters publicly vomited in red, white, and blue colors. The group called its action "a work of public art." In a flier, the painters said: "Look at the medium. Think about why it was chosen over conventional paint. Think about why Dan Quayle is visiting Portland. Look at our painting. Think about your government. Throw up your values." The colored vomit was created by ingesting mashed potatoes with either red, blue, or no food coloring mixed in. Then all took ipecac syrup or plain vinegar. One problem with the vomit was that for some reason the blue actually looked more greenish.

IN INDIA, 20,000 ANGRY FARMERS PRO-
testing the state government gathered outside the legislature building and laughed for two hours. M. D. Nanjundaswamy, leader of the Karnataka Farmers Association, explained, "We want to laugh this government out."

FOR YEARS THE STATE OF MONTANA HAS
donated road-killed deer, elk, moose, and bears to local food banks to feed the needy. However, beginning in the winter of 1992, many of the reported kills could not be found. Officials said they suspected that people listening in on police radio scanners had overheard the locations of road-kills and raced there first to pick it up for themselves before the state could retrieve it. "Most Montanans look at it and say, 'Gee, that's a good piece of meat and shouldn't go to waste,'" wildlife officer Ed Kelly explained, pointing out that the recession might have encouraged the pick-ups, which under state law are illegal.

New Hampshire holds an annual road-kill auction, which in 1992 included 30 black bears, a dozen bobcats, seven beavers, two coyotes, six otters, three wild turkeys, a grouse, several mink, a weasel, a raccoon, and a muskrat. Most of the animals showed minimal damage from collisions with vehicles. Most of the buyers were interested in fur for rugs, skulls for display, or the whole animal for taxidermy projects.

AUTHORITIES BLAMED A RASH OF COWS

being slaughtered in their fields in Stevens County, Washington, on hunger. "People are out of work" and not good hunters, said investigator Jerry Mugaas.

SCIENTISTS IN THE LATVIAN CAPITAL OF

Riga had to launch an education campaign warning people not to buy rabbits at local food markets after 42 laboratory rabbits infected with carcinogens and hepatitis were stolen. In the face of continued economic deterioration in the former Soviet Union in 1992, reports increased of animals being stolen from zoos, circuses, and research labs to be sold as food. In one incident, an art student was found by zoo officials in a polar bear's cage, stabbing the animal with a knife.

PETS IN THE '90S

• Japan's Takara Company began selling Mew, a fake cat that meows and wags its tail when it hears you speak. A spokesman for the company said that Mew "drives away loneliness." The company also introduced Baby Mew, a sleeping cat that "breathes" when touched.

• Sanwa Bank of Japan instituted savings accounts for "domesticated" animals. Pets banking there get account books with their names engraved on them and special notebooks to hold photos and personal data. The bank said that the accounts were created for those who "care about pets as members of their family." It suggested using the accounts to set aside money for such pet expenses as food, haircuts, health care, and funerals.

• Everlasting Memories Inc. of Dexter, Missouri, announced it would create a ceramic or porcelain statue of people's dead pets using the ashes of its cremated remains mixed in with the clay. Finished statues cost about $1,200. Susan McNeely Ellenbracht, founder of the company, suggested that the final product be about a foot high and weigh a couple pounds but said that the company can make any size depending on how much a customer wants to spend. The artist uses pictures of the pet and some of its hair for proper coloring.

• Recently introduced pet entertainment products included videos shot so as to capture the attention of cats and dogs. One notable tape, "Doggie Adventure" (Made-for-Dog-Video, $19.95), was a 25-minute sojourn through a variety of experiences all filmed from the point of view of a dog. A sequel is being filmed. Kitty Video (Lazy Cat Productions, $15) offers a cat 30 minutes of colorful birds chirping and moving around.

• Japanese veterinarians said they fear that many Japanese pet owners are transferring their stress to their cats and dogs. In response, Japan's Nippon Crown Co., which produces stress-relief music for people, began creating the same product for cats and dogs. Veterinarian Norio Aoki selected the especially composed and performed pieces of music after experimenting with dozens of samples on more than 100 cats and dogs. "Cheerful but serene music is good for dogs, and romantic music is good for cats," he said. "When they appreciated the music, [pets] approached the speakers and tilted their ears. About 20 to 30 minutes later, some cats even fell asleep." In its first month Nippon Crown sold 10,000 copies of the pet music CD at $17 each.

• Jackie Zajac and Shiela Mullan opened Fido's Fast Food, Toledo, Ohio's, only drive-through restaurant for dogs, featuring cheeseburgers, french fries, and peanut-butter bagels. All the food is dried and crunches. "My dog gave me the idea," said Zajac. "I would go through a drive-through and he would sit there and stare at me jealously. So we thought they should have their own restaurant."

IN DES MOINES, IOWA, CANUCK'S SPORTS-

man's Memorials announced a special offer for hunters. It would load their ashes into shotgun shells and shoot them at the animal of the deceased's choice.

FOLLOWING FINDINGS THAT ONE-FOURTH

of the 148 Americans killed in action in the Persian Gulf War were friendly-fire casualties, mostly by cannon shots from their own tanks, the Army announced that it would begin training tank gunners not to shoot their own troops by showing them a video that it had produced to help them tell one side from the other.

WHEN THE EUROPEAN COMMUNITY PRO-

posed a code governing sexual harassment in the workplace, a delegation of British women marched to EC headquarters in Brussels to voice their opposition. The women, all models who posed for British tabloids, feared the measure, which specifically bans nude pinups in the workplace, would cost them work.

IN SAN JOSE, CALIFORNIA, MICHAEL AND

Karen Graham were digging up a tree in the yard of their new $265,000 home in December when they discovered the whole hillside contained medical waste and trash. The state said the illegal dump would have to be removed and ordered the Grahams to pay the cleanup costs, which could exceed $1 million. "We fell in love with this house," Karen Graham lamented, "and now we're living on a landfill."

The Grahams bought the house a year earlier from Irene Pisciotta, 77, a nursing supervisor, who explained that she brought home intravenous tubes, syringes, kidney dialysis bags, and other medical waste from the nursing home where she worked from 1979 to 1988 and spread it in the backyard as fill to scare gophers and burglars. Neighbors added that they hadn't seen her take out any household trash in the 29 years she lived there.

UNIVERSITY OF WISCONSIN RESEARCH-

ers sent questionnaires to 1,200 Madison residents inquiring about their nose-picking habits. The first question asked was: "What finger do you use when picking your nose and after picking your nose how often do you find yourself looking at what you have removed?"

James Jefferson, a professor of psychiatry heading the study of rhinotillexomania, or chronic nose-picking, explained that the habit has never been scrutinized, but it has been linked to other impulse-control disorders such as hair-pulling and nail-biting. "Our assumption is that for most people, it is a harmless, private habit," he said. "But some may do it excessively in a way that causes embarrassment or social problems."

PERU'S CONSTITUTIONAL INTEGRATIONIST

Movement grew from 10 members to 300 in its first year, according to leader Fernando Quispe. The movement was formed to advocate the annexation of Peru by the United States, which would give it the status of an associated free state, like Puerto Rico. "We will have the privilege to taste different brands of soft drinks, paying no more than a dollar for each two-liter bottle," said Quispe, who acknowledged that there would be other benefits. "Our sons will immediately learn English for free, and they will have the opportunity to marry beautiful young American girls."

ACCEPT NO SUBSTITUTES

• A Japanese company, Japan Effectiveness Headquarters, provides rent-a-families for lunch and a few hours' conversation, according to China's Xinhua News Agency, which reported that elderly Japanese who miss their children can dial a Tokyo number and ask for a visit from actors posing as, "say, a daughter, son-in-law, and grandchild. They will show up at your door and greet you emotionally as if they haven't seen you in years." A three-hour visit costs $1,130 plus travel expenses. "We fill a hole in the heart," said JEH President Satuki Oiwa, who explained the service is popular with younger people too busy to visit their older relatives. JEH also provides make-believe " 'staff' for timid business executives to bawl out," "sweethearts" for those unlucky in love, and "maids" to make people feel rich.

• During a 1991 visit to Canada, British Princess Diana was scheduled to tour a brand-new heart wing at Ottawa Civic

Hospital. Because the heart unit had no patients yet, the hospital asked other former patients to return to the hospital, dress in pajamas, and lie in beds "to demonstrate to the princess what a day unit is."

• When Russian President Boris Yeltsin addressed a packed House of Commons during his visit to Ottawa in 1992, most of the audience that gave him two standing ovations weren't lawmakers, but stand-ins. According to a legislative staffer who requested anonymity, most of the members of parliament were out of town, so the seats were filled with parliamentary aides, committee clerks, House employees, and members of the prime minister's office.

THE NATIONAL MUSEUM IN HOLLAND

charged an American hired to restore its prized painting with ruining it by using a roller instead of a brush. Amsterdam's Stedelijk Museum said it sent Barnett Newman's abstract "Who's Afraid of Red, Yellow and Blue III" to Daniel Goldreyer of New York after vandals slashed the 18- by 8-foot oil painting in eight places. The 2½-year restoration cost $450,000. When the museum got its painting back, its own restorers questioned Goldreyer's work and had the Dutch Justice Ministry run tests, which concluded that Goldreyer painted over other areas of the canvas than the damaged spots he was supposed to touch up. They intimated that instead of duplicating the artist's painstaking pointillist technique with a narrow-tip brush, Goldreyer simply used an ordinary household paint roller.

Goldreyer denied the charges, saying the museum's restorers were just jealous. He blamed them for making him the victim of their "three-ring circus."

SPONSORS HAD TO CANCEL THEIR AN-
nual bicycle race around the island of Cuba in 1992 because
of a critical shortage of gasoline. Citing the virtual shutdown
of trade with the former Soviet bloc for the shortage, Jose
Pelaez explained that the gas would have been needed to
transport racers, staff, and equipment during the race.

IT'S ART, YOU PHILISTINE!

• James Wilkinson, 34, told Los Angeles police that he attached a 15-foot wooden cross to the "Y" of the "Hollywood"
sign, decorated it with plastic Christmas wreaths, a U.S.
flag, empty beer cans, and cigarette boxes and then climbed
onto the cross and strapped himself to it because "art speaks
for itself." Wilkinson, a musician who performs under the
name Jizzo Pearl, was charged with trespassing. Lieutenant
Charles Roper explained, "Everybody's trying to get their
15 minutes."
• Inspired by what the Los Angeles smog did to her Honda
Civic's windshield every day, artist Kim Abeles began laying paper stencils on sheets of Plexiglas and leaving them
outdoors to collect car exhaust, factory emissions, and barbecue smoke. Abeles then mounted the "smog collectors"
onto sculptures made out of tailpipes and mufflers. The California Bureau of Automotive Repair commissioned seven
pieces of her art for $15,000. Art collectors have paid be-
tween $300 and $5,700 for each of her works.
• Shinichi Kitahara arranged 180 little wooden triangles on
a grassy knoll for his senior art project at Texas Christian
University. Before his work could be graded, two workers

assigned to mow the lawn gathered up the triangles and stacked them beside a trash bin for disposal, according to John Dial, supervisor of the parks and recreation department crew. He explained that his men "evidently didn't recognize that as art. If it had been one large sculpture, I'm sure that mistake would not have been made."

• Theodore Waddell, a rancher-artist from Montana, created his "True Objects and Stories from Two Dot" exhibit out of cow skulls and road-kill. When it was put on exhibit at the Fine Art Gallery at the Cheney Cowles Museum in Spokane, Washington, exterminators had to be called in to deal with a black fly problem it had generated. Among other things, his work contained a flattened coyote stretched across a canvas and a smashed rabbit mounted on a canvas and covered with psychedelic paint.

• Jason Brewer unveiled his artwork "Out of Sight, Out of Mind," consisting of an 8-foot wall of filing cabinets wrapped with red tape into which he had tossed bags of stinking garbage. Brewer, 22, a student at Kendall College of Art and Design in Grand Rapids, Michigan, explained, "We just send all our garbage out to compost heaps and dumps out in the country and forget about it." Just hours after its week-long exhibition started, it had to be removed from the gallery due to the stench.

• A Cook County, Illinois, jury ruled that Themis Klotz's front yard was in violation of health and fire codes. The yard held her work of art, which she had titled "The Monument to Humanity No One Will Be Left to Build After George Bush Has His Winnable Limited Protracted Nuclear War With 20 Million Americans Acceptable Loss." The artwork consisted of a Pontiac station wagon buried under 44 tons of sand, orange snow fencing, a dolphin-print T-shirt, moldy books, lawn chairs, a rusty gas tank, a spare tire, a pencil, a Christmas tree, and a carton of Ben & Jerry's Rainforest Crunch ice cream.

• Orlando, Florida, police arrested GG Allin, 35, lead singer of GG and the Murder Junkies, after a performance by the band at an Orlando club. According to witnesses, Allin began the show by smashing a bottle over his head and grinding the glass into his forehead. Later he urinated and defecated on stage, then he and a fellow band member ate some of the feces and began throwing it at the crowd. "Every time he went to one side of the club everyone ran to the other side," said one audience member. Allin has been arrested for many performances (50 or 60 times according to his producer) while performing with several of his former bands, including the Scumfucs, the Jabbers, and AIDS Brigade. He has released a cassette titled "Hate Is in the Nation."

• Artist Lee Brozgold's exhibit at The Dance Theater Workshop in New York City in late 1991 was titled "40 Patriots/ Countless Americans." It consisted of papier-mâché "death masks" of such people as George and Barbara Bush, Ronald and Nancy Reagan, Dan and Marilyn Quayle, David Duke, Neil Bush, Oliver North, Arnold Schwarzenegger, and 30 others. Brozgold said that his subjects "represent the old order. They're outdated. . . . They should be dead. . . . The whole thesis of this exhibit is that these people . . . are opposed to recognizing the rights of what I call common Americans."

THE SPORT OF KINGS

Bruce Kaufman, executive director of the U.S. Lawn Mower Racing Association, said: "Double the speed at which you

normally ride and throw a bunch of other mower maniacs
on the track with you, and it could be white-knuckle city."

LANDSCAPING ROOM

German officials announced discovery of a grove of trees
shaped like a swastika near the eastern town of Zernikow.
The grove extends more than 100 yards, but its shape can
be detected only from the air. The trees, noticed by Guenter
Reschke, a regional government official, while looking
through four-year-old aerial photographs, apparently were
planted in the mid-1930s by the Hitler Youth.

BRITISH RAIL SPENT IN EXCESS OF

$350,000 to install an all-weather canopy over the platform
at its Penzance station, but because the fumes from the diesel trains couldn't escape the new canopy, passengers were
directed to board and leave the trains from an unprotected
section of the platform. "Arriving trains stop as normal inside the station," a British Rail spokesperson explained.
"The engine is then shut down. A second engine is then
attached to the rear of the arriving train. The engine tows
the train out of the canopy area to the new alighting-
departing fume-free platform."

UNABLE TO GET THE CITY OF TULSA,

Oklahoma, to pay delinquent taxes on some municipal property, the treasurer of Tulsa County ordered 11 tracts auctioned, including a 24-acre strip of land the city bought in
1985 for $1.5 million. The county got $200 for it.

The Everett, Washington, School District decided that a statue hanging on a school cafeteria wall for 10 years was a safety hazard and removed it. Declaring the 48-foot-long sculpture surplus, the district auctioned it off to Nick Agostinelli for $25. Afterward, the school district discovered the sculpture actually was part of a state art collection and was worth $13,000. Agostinelli said he would sell the work back to the school district for $2,500, explaining, "I'm strictly in this game for profit."

WORKERS AT THE UNITED NATIONS' EUropean headquarters in Geneva were directed to stop drinking before lunchtime. An official announcement notified workers that alcoholic beverages would no longer be served in the U.N.'s bars and restaurants before 11:30 A.M.

WHEN FRENCH INTERIOR MINISTER PHI-lippe Marchand banned dwarf-tossing in November, calling the bar sport an "intolerable attack on human dignity" and exploitation of the handicapped, 3-foot-11 Manuel Wackenheim promptly sued, claiming his promising career as a professional projectile ($1,800 on a good night) had been cut short.

MANY TELEVISION STATIONS ARE TRYING to fulfill requirements of the Children's Television Act of 1990 by showing cartoons and situation comedies, according to a report prepared by the Center for Media Education and the Institute for Public Representation of Georgetown University Law Center. The act requires broadcasters to provide programs "specifically designed" to educate and inform children, but some stations are simply using sociological and educational terms to describe standard cartoons and vintage comedies. "Many broadcasters are coming up with new descriptions of old programs rather than finding new programs to meet the mandate of the law," said the report.

One New Orleans station, for example, said the animated "Bucky O'Hare" meets the federal requirements because "good-doer Bucky fights off the evil toads from aboard his ship. Issues of social consciousness and responsibility are central themes of program."

Other examples of shows that local TV stations have submitted as "educational and informational programming" under the act:

"Leave It to Beaver": "Eddie misunderstands Wally's help to his girlfriend, Cindy, and confronts Wally with his fist. Communication and trust are shown in this episode."

"James Bond Jr." (cartoon): "Junior secret service agent fights for good against evil. Many of the episodes feature information on geography. . . . Some story lines include science information."

"GI Joe" (cartoon): "The Joes fight against an evil that has capabilities of mass destruction of society. Issues of social consciousness and responsibility are show themes."

The report noted that some stations are airing new syndicated informational and educational programs more in line with the act's intent, although 60 percent of them are scheduled between 5:30 A.M. and 7 A.M., times virtually inaccessible to the young audiences they are intended to reach.

ITALIAN ART CRITICS HAILED THE DECI-

sion by Fabrizio Mancinelli, director of the restoration of Michelangelo's 16th-century Sistine Chapel fresco "Last Judgment," to keep the loincloths that were added to the dramatic work after some church officials expressed shock at Michelangelo's nude figures. Leading art historian Giulio Carlo Argan said the modest adornments by Daniele da Volterra, ordered in 1564 by Pope Pius IV, "document an episode of history."

WHITE-COLLAR HELL

The Roman Catholic Church published its first fully revised catechism in four centuries, updating its list of sins to reflect the temptations of the modern world. Among the new acts and behavior said to put one's soul in jeopardy are drunken driving, failing to vote, evading income taxes, forging checks, fraudulent accounting, corporate embezzlement, bribery, charging unjust rents, paying unfair salaries, wasting resources, discriminating on the basis of sex, sexual orientation, age, religion, national origin or handicap, doing shoddy work, artificially manipulating markets to inflate prices, mistreating the environment, abusing or trafficking in drugs, and genetic engineering. Prostitution and suicide remain sins, but the new catechism acknowledges that people may be driven to them by desperation or particularly cruel social circumstances. The new "Universal Catechism" also directs Catholics to avoid astrologers, fortune-tellers, and seances.

A BUSINESS IN HANGZHOU, CHINA, PAID

$23,450 for the mobile telephone number 901688 at an auction, the China News Service reported. In Chinese, the number 1688 sounds like "get rich continuously." The price topped the previous record of $20,000 for a phone number, set just the week before, at an auction in Qingdao.

ON THE HEELS OF SERIAL KILLER TRADING

cards, a Long Island company unveiled "sex maniac" trading card sets featuring Mike Tyson, Elvis Presley, Catherine the Great, and others, described by First Amendment Publishing Inc. as "the most twisted and bizarre sex offenders ever." The company said that Presley, who lived with 15-year-old Priscilla Beaulieu, appears on a "rock 'n' roll cradle-robbers card" that includes Chuck Berry, Jerry Lee Lewis, and Bill Wyman.

Meanwhile, Comic Zone Productions of Berlin, New Jersey, released a series of "Psycho Killer" comics, featuring the misdeeds of mass murderer Charles Manson, "Son of Sam" killer David Berkowitz, Milwaukee butcher Jeffrey Dahmer, and Ed Gein, whose grisly exploits inspired the movie "Psycho."

DESPITE THE APPARENT END OF THE COLD

war, Swiss government ministers proceeded with plans to build a nuclear bomb shelter. They voted to spend $104.6 million to complete the shelter, which is designed to house the seven members of the ruling Federal Council and their aides. Switzerland also plans to build enough shelters for its entire population of 6.8 million people.

THE U.S. GOVERNMENT HAS 32 BILLION

cubic feet of helium stored beneath 20 square miles of Texas Panhandle in case of an outbreak of blimp warfare. Established by Congress in 1929, when blimps were expected to be the war machines of the future, the National Helium Reserves was renewed in 1960 and ordered to boost stockpiles of the lighter-than-air gas. In 1973 Congress decided the nation had enough helium to keep U.S. blimps in the air and ordered the Bureau of Mines, which runs the program, to maintain the existing supply. The program was budgeted to cost $22 million to operate in 1993. Even though it expects to cover this sum by selling off small amounts of helium to other government agencies, since it borrowed money to start the operation and buy the helium, the debt now exceeds $1 billion and annual interest payments are almost $130 million. Its principal customers, NASA and the Defense and Energy Departments, are required by law to buy from the reserve, but must pay more than they would if they bought from private suppliers.

PARTS, JUST PARTS

• Noting that the increasing number of shooting deaths in Los Angeles has made more organs and other body parts available for transplants, Donald Ward, executive director of the Lions' Doheny Eyebank, observed: "Homicides are a terrible thing, but some good can come out of them."
• Organ traders in Argentina are paying donors $2,000 for kidneys and charging desperate patients up to $45,000. Some merchants reportedly raid slums in search of young donors, and even kidnap some.
• Russian clinics that once treated the Communist Party elite began making the transition to private medicine by offering cheap services to foreigners, especially cut-rate organs. "Kidney transplants seem to be their favorite," said Dr. Anatoly Mironyenko, deputy head of a city commission

investigating the sale of organs in Moscow. "Figures such as $40,000 are being quoted. By world levels this is a dumping price."

• In an attempt to crack down on a flourishing black market for human kidneys, the Egyptian Society of Nephrology banned the transplant of kidneys from donors unrelated to patients and urged Parliament to pass legislation that would allow kidneys taken from cadavers to be used. Before banning kidney transplants between living donors who aren't related, Egypt had become a leading seller of organs, particularly kidneys, over the previous 11 years. The city's six kidney transplant centers were doing about 350 operations a year. Most patients were wealthy Arabs from Egypt's Persian Gulf neighbors, whose own countries do not have such vast numbers of poor willing to sell their organs. According to Dr. Rashad Barsoum, secretary-general of the Egyptian Society of Kidney Specialists, private laboratories often act as brokerage houses, recruiting donors from the slums and charging buyers $10,000 to $15,000, just for the organ itself. Reports also said that poverty-stricken donors actually held kidney auctions, selling theirs to the highest bidder.

IN PHOENIX, ARIZONA, NEW BILINGUAL

signs put up at Sky Harbor International Airport to help visitors from Mexico were riddled with incorrect words, misspellings, mixed tenses, and genders. One sign intended to warn arriving travelers who don't declare plants, fruits, vegetables, and meats that they would be fined, instead read "Violadores Seran Finados" ("Violators Will Be Deceased"). Another sign, announcing the drinking age, omitted a tilde in the word "ano," changing its meaning from "year" to "anus." City Manager Frank Fairbanks admitted, "The airport hired a poor translator."

WHEN FRED TURNER'S PICKUP TRUCK

broke down while he was vacationing in South Carolina, he decided to walk home to Sparks, Nevada. "I weighed the pros and cons," Turner said, "and the only con I could find was that some people would think I was crazy."

The 53-year-old man announced that he would walk across America to prove that most people are good. Eight days later, while he was walking across a bridge from South Carolina to Georgia, two men pulled alongside him in a pickup truck and asked if he was the guy walking across America. Turner said, "I told them yes and they said, 'Good, give me your wallet.'"

After taking $480, his right shoe, hat, and walking stick, they pushed him off the bridge into the Savannah River. Weighed down by his backpack, he drifted with the current to a nearby island, where he spent the night before two fishermen rescued him.

Undaunted, he continued his journey, arriving in Carlsbad, California, five months later. He said the journey reaffirmed his belief that 99 percent of people are good.

IN INDIA, SUDHAKAR RAO NAIK, CHIEF

minister of the heavily populated state of Maharashtra, proposed that jobs in government and public companies be denied to parents with more than two children. To control India's burgeoning population, Naik also recommended that anyone in elected office who has a third child be forced to resign.

AUTHORITIES IN TAOS COUNTY, NEW MEX-

ico, said that Andrew Casados, 25, a specialized "hotshot" firefighter for the U.S. Forest Service, killed his father-in-law, Albert Martinez, 58, by dousing him with gasoline and setting him on fire. Casados, who confronted Martinez looking for his missing wife, also died in the inferno.

POLICE IN COLUMBIA, MISSISSIPPI,

charged Tina Ward, 33, with setting her 15-year-old son on fire after she found him sniffing gasoline. According to the sheriff, the boy died after Ward "apparently poured the gas on the boy and struck a lighter to him."

IN LEADVILLE, COLORADO, CHRIS ROGERS,

20, was shampooing his hair with gasoline to rid himself of head lice when the gas exploded. According to Assistant Fire Chief Greg Stanley of the Leadville-Lake County Fire Department, Rogers suffered second-degree burns over half his body when vapors from the gasoline were ignited by the pilot light in a wall heater.

SENIOR BUREAUCRATS IN SINGAPORE BE-

gan taking singing lessons after Prime Minister Goh Chok Tong announced that he wanted Singaporeans to be socially confident overseas and able to sing if called on by their hosts. More than 300 civil servants signed up for a workshop called "When Asked to Sing, I Can." The official repertoire includes the Carpenters' "Sing" and "Top of the World", and Henry Mancini's "Moon River."

BERKELEY, CALIFORNIA, IMPOSED A TAX

on church collections. The Finance Department of the financially strapped city sent notices telling churches and other nonprofit groups that they must get business licenses and pay an annual tax of 60 cents on every $1,000 in contributions.

THE U.S. SUPREME COURT STRUCK DOWN

the principle of "finders, keepers." The ruling came in the case of salvagers who in 1987 recovered up to $1 billion in gold from a ship that sank in a hurricane off South Carolina in 1857. Half the 16 British and U.S. companies that insured the vessel were still in business and filed a claim for a share of the treasure. The unanimous ruling stunned explorers and treasure hunters, who said it would prevent their undertaking costly expeditions to recover lost treasure.

IN BATON ROUGE, LOUISIANA, JAPANESE

high school exchange student Yoshihiro Hattori, 16, was shot to death when he knocked on Rodney Peairs's door and was greeted with the shouted order, "Freeze," which he did not understand. Police said he moved and was shot. The American Field Service, an organization that brings exchange students from Japan, responded to the incident by updating the slang taught in its orientation lessons, according to the *Japan Digest*. New phrases include: "Don't move," "Hands up," "Halt," "Cool it," and "Chill out."

A 1992 POLL FOUND THAT MOST CZECHS

considered love to be the main reason that life is worth living, according to a new poll. The second most popular reason given was the thought of kicking separatist Slovak Prime Minister Vladimir Meciar in the rear end.

A NORWEGIAN ARTIST PROPOSED TURN-

ing 43,000 tanks, which were being scrapped by European governments as part of a sweeping arms reduction plan, into a giant peace monument along the Polish-German border. The monument would be six-tenths of a mile long and several stories high.

REHABILITATION PROJECTS

• Japan's biggest crime syndicate issued a code of conduct, according to police. The 30,000-member Yamaguchi-gumi's six-point good-conduct code, implemented to avoid running afoul of a new law against organized crime, bans new recruits from throwing cigarette butts on the ground, making grand entries into hotels, trains, or golf courses, or giving out business cards with the gang's symbol. A gang spokesperson explained to the *Mainichi Shimbun* newspaper, "The basic idea is not to inconvenience the public."

• The crime syndicate also threatened a court challenge to the new anti-organized crime law. Makoto Endo, chief lawyer for the Yamaguchi-gumi gang, explained that its designation by the National Safety Commission as a "violence group" violates the human rights of its members.

• A Japanese plastic surgeon approached police, offering his

services to Yakuza gangsters who renounce crime. According to the *Mainichi Shimbun* newspaper, the surgeon replaces a gangster's ritually severed finger, the mark of membership in the Yakuza crime syndicate, with a little toe.
• Rehabilitation programs for Swedish convicts include teaching them skills that make it easier for them to escape, according to a member of parliament. Criticizing a program where inmates are given shotguns so they can learn skeet shooting, Gothe Knutson complained to Justice Minister Gun [sic] Hellsvik: "Armed prisoners might decide to ignore the clay pigeons and turn the weapons on their guards." Knutson also condemned another "crazy education project" he said might encourage prisoners to scale walls by taking them to the mountains to teach them how to climb with ropes. Hellsvik's predecessor, Leila Freivalds, once stated that it would be inhuman for any prisoner to feel there was no chance of escape.

WHEN JAMES BATEMAN, 14, WAS SENT home from school in Colorado City, Arizona, for wearing a T-shirt depicting the Penguin, a character in the movie *Batman Returns*, the boy's mother, Trudie Bateman, met with principal Lawrence Steed. She said that when she asked Steed why the shirt was inappropriate, he explained, "It's a sign of devil worship." After actor Danny DeVito, who played the character, read about the incident, he sent the teenager more Penguin merchandise.

ROBERT MICHAEL HERSCH, CHAIRMAN OF a Tucson, Arizona, cable television company, suspended a public access program called "The Great Satan at Large" while Pima County authorities determined whether it violated obscenity and hate-crime laws and should be banned. Reacting to a public outcry after one show featured profanity, nudity, ethnic and racial slurs, and explicit discussion and depiction of sex acts, Hersch imposed a 90-day suspension, describing the show, hosted by "The Great Satan" and "Satan's Jester," as "sort of a talk show, but it's definitely not the 'Johnny Carson Show.'"

THE ARCHITECTURAL AND TRANSPORTA-

tion Barriers Compliance Board, an independent federal agency whose members are appointed by the president, decreed that all bank automated teller machines, which cost banks $3.1 billion, must be made accessible to the visually impaired to comply with the Americans with Disabilities Act. The order included drive-up ATMs.

TO IMPROVE SAFETY STANDARDS AT THE

Rocky Flats, Colorado, nuclear weapons plant, managers of the facility revised the procedure for changing a light bulb in a criticality beacon, which warns workers of spontaneous nuclear accidents. Replacing the bulb, which used to be a 12-step process that took 12 workers 4.15 hours to complete, became a 33-step procedure that takes at least 43 people 1,087.1 hours to complete.

The steps call for a lead planner to meet with six other people at a work-control meeting; talk with other workers who have done the job before; meet again; get signatures from five people at the work-control meeting; get the project plans approved by separate officials overseeing safety, logistics, environmental, maintenance, operations, waste management, and plant scheduling; wait for a

monthly criticality beacon test; direct electricians to replace
the bulb; and then test and verify the repair.

A WOMAN CALLED POLICE TO REPORT

seeing an armed robber at a video store in Lilly, Pennsylvania, but when officers entered the store with guns drawn,
manager Kelly Miller told them there was no robbery. Police solved the mystery when the woman realized she had
mistaken a life-size movie poster cutout of gun-toting actor
Denzel Washington from the police thriller *Ricochet* for the
gunman.

NEW-AGE KOSHER

• Jews forbidden from eating or drinking on Yom Kippur,
the Day of Atonement, may take appetite suppressant pills
before the fast to help them resist eating, according to
Rabbi Yona Metzger, pastor to Tel Aviv's fashionable northern suburbs. Although self-denial and discomfort are part of
the individual's atonement, Metzger explained that the pills
would reduce the "anguish" but not the "torture" of not
eating.
• When their apartment in Bnei Brak, Israel, started burning, tenants asked a rabbi whether the fire constituted an
emergency so they could break the Sabbath and use the
telephone to call the fire department. The rabbi considered
the matter for 30 minutes, during which the blaze spread to
two neighboring apartments. The rabbi decided the tenants
could call firefighters, but by the time they arrived all three
buildings were gutted.
• A coalition of Jews, Muslims, and Seventh Day Adventists

persuaded major U.S. steelmakers to produce kosher steel. Rabbi Jonah Gewirtz of Silver Spring, Maryland, formed the coalition after discovering that steel used to make cans routinely is coated during processing with lubricants containing animal fats. Even after cleaning, analysis showed, steel retained some of the oil. When made aware of the situation, most of the container and steel companies began switching to non-animal lubricants. Gerwitz and his colleagues formed a company that will charge steelmakers a fee for kosher certification. He estimated the first-year revenues could approach $700,000.

• In Sandusky, Ohio, rabbi Samuel Eidelman, 24, was shot in the abdomen by rabbi Avrohom Greenberg, 31, with a harpoon gun used to kill cattle at a meat-packing plant. Police ruled the shooting was an accident, explaining that Greenberg found the non-kosher stunning device where the rabbis kept their knives and was trying to unjam it when it discharged, shooting a 4-inch retractable rod. "We never use the stunning device. We only kill kosher," Greenberg said, explaining he considered the gun "cruel to animals."

• Israel's chief rabbi, Mordechai Eliahu, ruled that Jews should not take U.S. dollars out of their pockets when they are in a restroom or other unclean places. The rabbi explained that because the bills have the slogan "In God We Trust" printed on them, they must be treated the same as holy documents and not be exposed to filth.

ARIZONA ORDERED THAT PRISONERS BE-ing executed must strip to their underwear before entering the gas chamber. When family members of some death-row inmates decried the policy as unnecessary humiliation, Mike Arra, spokesperson for the Department of Corrections, explained that it is a safety precaution because the cyanide

gas used can collect in clothing, creating a hazard for the prison crew that removes the body.

JAPAN ANNOUNCED THAT IT WAS SEND-

ing Korea 20,000 noses. Japanese forces cut them off as proof of kills during their invasion of Korea in 1597. The noses turned up in 1983 after years of searching by South Korean university professor Kim Moon-gil and Buddhist monk Park Sam-joong, who discovered them in a tomb in Japan. Reports said the noses would be officially welcomed home in a special ceremony.

THE U.S. BUREAU OF PRISONS AN-

nounced that federal inmates would have to pay for their incarceration. The user fee, approved by Congress to offset rising prison costs, is to equal the average cost of one year's incarceration, estimated at between $17,000 and $20,000. Officials estimated that the fee would raise $49 million a year, once they figure out how to collect it.

LACK OF MONEY BY POLAND'S PRISON

system forced one institution with overdue bills for food and fuel to cut phone service, remove radios from prisoners' cells, and begin charging inmates a fee for using their own televisions.

TRUE SEX

• Sex was invented 1.1 billion years ago, scientists have discovered. It began, they explained, when single-cell plankton developed pores that allowed sex cells to be released into the ocean. Citing diversity among plankton fossils that they analyzed, paleobiologists J. William Schopf of the University of California at Los Angeles and Carl Mendelson of Beloit College in Wisconsin noted that until the origin of sexual reproduction, which combined characteristics of both parents, asexually begotten offspring were genetic copies of previous generations.

• Today, people have sex at least 100 million times a day, the World Health Organization reported. "I think it might be an underestimation," admitted Dr. Mahmoud Fathalla, author of the WHO report, who computed the figure by multiplying the world birth rate by the accepted estimate of the number of times sex does not result in conception. "It is not the outcome of a survey we have carried out worldwide to find out how much fun is going on in the world."

Even so:

• During an extended drought in the North African nation of Niger, police arrested 16 people after catching them having sex in dried-up cattle troughs. Police acted against the couples after Muslim clerics in Nkonni village complained that "illicit" activities were hampering the effectiveness of collective prayers for rain.

• After engaging in oral sex in a first-class compartment aboard a train from Margate, England, to London, a couple moved to a packed second-class compartment and, according to authorities, performed "full sexual intercourse." Other passengers ignored them—until they had finished and lit cigarettes. Several annoyed passengers complained to the conductor that the compartment was designated non-smoking. Police met the train and arrested John Henderson, 29, and Zoe D'Arcy, 19, who were each fined $142 for violating the smoking regulation and committing an indecent act.

• After 50 years of communist-imposed morality, Albania was flooded with pornography in the wake of liberation. In addition, most newspapers began publishing nude photographs, and the literary magazine *Drita* began devoting a page to the sex life of foreign personalities.

• Doctors at Bulgaria's Kozloduy nuclear plant found that workers were being exposed to above-average levels of radiation. They also concluded that the higher radiation boosted the workers' sex drive. Kozloduy psychiatrist Galina Palieva noted that increased potency had been observed among workers exposed to radiation and that wife-swapping at the sprawling complex was rife.

• Scientists, discovering crocodiles moving north from their nesting sites at the southern tip of Florida, concluded that the Florida Power & Light Turkey Point nuclear plant just south of Miami had created ideal breeding conditions for the once-endangered animal, causing them to breed rapidly and spread as far north as Fort Lauderdale, where they hadn't been seen in years.

• After failing to get a female gorilla at Japan's Hamamatsu City Zoo pregnant because she and her mate didn't have sex often enough, her keepers started showing her video-tapes of wild gorillas mating to arouse her. "The problem is that there aren't that many videos showing gorillas having sex," veterinarian Rikio Nakazawa explained. "If there were a porno video of gorillas, we'd really like to get our hands on it."

• In Harfsen, Netherlands, a 2,640-pound bull named Sunny Boy produced his 1 millionth dose of semen, a feat widely believed to be unequaled in cattle breeding, according to Ronald van Giessen, head of the KI Oost cattle-breeding cooperative. Van Giessen said the seven-year-old bull could be the father of as many as 600,000 calves.

• In an investigation of the bull semen business for Canadian Press, Stuart Laidlaw reported that stud bulls "are fixed with plastic vaginas and taught to mount beef steers (cas-trated males), which are used instead of dairy cows because they can better withstand constant mounting."

• Boston psychiatrist Albert Gaw identified a condition called "koro," which strikes mostly Chinese and Southeast Asian men, causing the victims to believe their genitals are shrinking. Koro epidemics in China have caused victims to use strings, clamps, and even tight-gripped friends to keep their organs from disappearing.

• Miami surgeon Ricardo Samitier told *Cosmopolitan* mag-azine that he could add both length and thickness to men's penises by suctioning fat from the lower abdomen and in-jecting it into the organ. He said that his procedure "dra-matically improves self-esteem."

• A surgeons' group investigated reports that the chief surgeon at a Shriners Burn Institute drew "happy faces" on the penises of two patients. After being cleared, the doctor explained that he drew the faces to relieve the patients' stress. "That was a joke between me and him with the smiley face," one patient said. "I'll let him draw another anytime."

• Noting that some 250,000 of the 10.7 million U.S. women who take oral contraceptives become pregnant because they fail to follow directions properly, the federal government asked the makers of birth control pills to standardize and simplify instructions. A Food and Drug Administration letter suggested, for instance, that a current set of directions telling users "contraceptive efficacy should not be assumed until after the first seven consecutive days of administration" be changed to "use another method of birth control as a backup method from the Sunday you start your first pack until the next Sunday."

• Authorities accused two staff members at New York's Mount Sinai Medical Center of running an unlicensed sperm bank in which they were the only donors. The state Department of Health investigation found that from October 1989 to January 1992, medical resident Douglas Moss and center medical school lab director Jerald H. Tedeschi earned $9,000 by selling their semen to four doctors to use to artificially inseminate at least 17 women.

• Fourteen death-row inmates in California filed a lawsuit in U.S. District Court asking the state to allow them to father children through conjugal visits or artificial insemination. One of the inmates named in the suit, Herbert J. Coddington, was sentenced to death for killing his two children in a custody dispute with his wife.

According to the inmates' attorney, Carter R. King, laws banning prisoners from procreating constitute cruel and unusual punishment. Acknowledging that the Supreme

Court has denied past requests for conjugal visits for condemned inmates, citing security, King noted, "Obviously, artificial insemination doesn't create a security risk."

• Despite the world's largest population, mandatory family planning (one child per couple) and one of the longest traditions of erotic literature, China has many well-educated people who don't know how babies are made, according to Jiang Yunfen, vice president of the Shanghai Sex Education Research Society. "We've had childless college professors who come in after being married for several years," she said, "and they still believe that if they just lie down together and fall asleep, they will produce a baby." The society had earlier sponsored the city's first public sex-education exhibit, which featured tiny clay figures demonstrating four love-making positions.

• The Australian government ordered a brothel in South Australia to set up a training program for its employees or pay penalties. Under Australian law, any company with sales over a certain amount must spend 1 percent of the total take on training.

• The Australian Federation of AIDS organizations announced it was seeking donations of used dildos to replace carrots and bananas being used in sex education programs in developing nations. Sponsors admitted that produce wasn't getting the point across.

• Valery V. Karpov, a city councillor in Astrakhan, Russia, proposed that the city build a special youth hotel with hourly bedroom rates so young people who want to have sex don't have to use stairwells and cemeteries. When the measure met a storm of protest from citizens accustomed to communist puritanism, Karpov responded, "What I proposed is nothing more than the sort of purpose motels in America are put to."

• Dan Patrick, general manager of Houston radio station

KSEV, broadcast his regular morning talk show while undergoing a vasectomy.

• Finally and everlastingly, there is no sex in heaven. Pope John Paul II proclaimed so while visiting a parish in Rome. Residents don't miss it, he explained, because "they are like the angels."

Technology to the Rescue

EVEN BETTER THAN THE REAL THING

The U.S. Geological Survey paid Cemrock Landscapes Inc. $6,000 to install two fake boulders at the bottom of the Grand Canyon. The hollow polyester-and-fiberglass rocks, 5 feet and 4 feet high, hide a water-sampling station.

THE JAPANESE GOVERNMENT AN-nounced it was funding a two-year, $4-million research project to take 180 measurements from 50,000 people to determine the size of the average Japanese head, shoulders, knees, toes, and more. According to the Research Institute of Human Engineering for Quality Life, which is supervising the project, the data will be used to set government standards and could help private businesses determine the best sizes for everything from toilet seats to the rings that standing commuters hold while riding trains.

GUY BALFOUR OF CORTEZ, COLORADO,

started a business to remove pesky prairie dogs from urban areas or on farms by using a powerful vacuum system. The prairie dogs are sucked from their burrows up a tube 4 inches in diameter and 50 feet long, then slide along a padded deflector plate and are dumped into a tank in his truck alive, he said, "but somewhat confused." He revealed that the idea for the business came to him in a dream.

RESEARCHERS AT THE GEORGIA INSTI-

tute of Technology built a stereo system the size of a room so they can observe the effects of sonic booms on people inside their homes. The institute explained that for its 12-month study, sponsored by NASA, volunteers would sit in a small house next to the giant speakers blaring sonic booms.

POULTRY SCIENTISTS IN TAIWAN RE-

ported success using acupuncture to prevent broodiness in hens, a condition in which the hen sits on her egg to hatch it instead of laying more eggs. The treatment involves inserting a needle into the hen's head between the nostrils on the beak and leaving it there for two days.

GEORGE M. WHITE OF BIRMINGHAM, MI-

chigan, received a patent for a mask that he said removes odors from the breath of hunters and makes it far more difficult for the deer to detect their presence.

LOW CHOLESTEROL MAY BE AS DEADLY

as high levels, according to a report in the *Archives of Internal Medicine*. Citing a 12-year study of 350,000 middle-aged American men, the report noted that the 6 percent with the lowest cholesterol were least likely to die of heart disease. The same people, however, were twice as likely to die of intercranial hemorrhage, three times as likely to have liver cancer, twice as likely to die of lung disease, twice as likely to commit suicide, and five times as likely to die of alcoholism.

Dr. Thomas Price, a stroke researcher at the University of Maryland Medical Center in Baltimore, reacted to the findings by noting that alcoholics with liver disease would be expected to have low cholesterol. He added that he was especially intrigued by the apparent link between low cholesterol, suicide, and homicide.

A TWO-YEAR-OLD NEWSLETTER SENT TO

thousands of dentists by the Princeton Dental Resource Center reported that research showed chocolate could fight cavity-causing plaque. Following this claim, newspapers reported that the center in Trenton, New Jersey, which isn't affiliated with Princeton University, receives 90 percent of its funding from the candy company M&M-Mars. The center offered dentists who put it in their waiting room chances to win free round-trip airfare to an American Dental Association convention. Issues frequently mentioned possible dental and general health benefits of chocolate, although the connection with the candy company wasn't disclosed.

The author of the study cited, Dr. Lawrence Wolinsky at the University of California at Los Angeles, said the newsletter misrepresented his work. He had written only that certain elements in cocoa can inhibit the development of plaque, not as the newsletter stated that eating candy bars in moderation "might even inhibit cavities."

WORRYING ABOUT SURGERY MAY BE

good for patients, according to researchers who measured stress-hormone levels of patients before and after abdominal surgery. Some listened to relaxation tapes before their operation, others didn't. Reported in the journal *Psychosomatic Medicine*, the study suggested that patients who worry before surgery may undergo less physical stress than patients who start out more relaxed. "Most doctors go to a lot of trouble to reassure their patients and reduce their stress. Our results show that might actually be harmful," said Peter Salmon, doctor of psychology at University College in London. "In the future, we may advise doctors not to reassure patients."

Dr. Thomas Hunt of the University of California at San Francisco reacted to the study by saying, "In the long run, surgery is something a patient should worry about."

U.S. DEPARTMENT OF AGRICULTURE RE-

searchers announced that they identified the molecule that gives fine cuts of beef their distinctive taste. Arthur Spanier, an animal physiologist at the USDA's research center

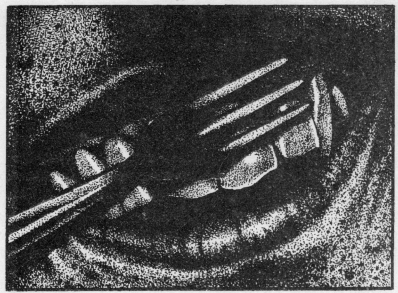

in New Orleans, explained that the material, called BMP for beefy-meaty peptide, could be used to make cheaper cuts of beef taste like prime cuts and to turn chicken, fish, leftovers, and soybeans into ersatz steak.

BEING SHORT IS AN ILLNESS IN NEED OF

a cure, according to the National Institutes of Health, which began treating hundreds of short children using genetically engineered human growth hormone. Critics of the NIH program argued that it is unethical to subject children to more than 150 shots a year of a drug with unclear side effects simply because they don't meet social norms. "These kids have no medical problem," said Jeremy Rifkin, president of the Foundation for Economic Trends, a biotechnology watchdog group, "they're just short kids."

THE JAPANESE COMPANY HITACHI MET-

als developed a way of holding false teeth in place by using a magnet and a small, stainless-steel plate embedded in the roof of the mouth. Noting that the company initially was concerned that the magnet would attract forks, spoons, and other metal objects, a Hitachi spokesperson said the system "is perfectly designed so as to stop the magnet from attracting anything except false teeth." He added that the company tested the product's safety by trying it on rabbits.

(According to a study by Dr. Toby Litovitz in the journal *Pediatrics*, iron supplements are the biggest cause of accidental poisoning deaths in children under 6, who often mistake the iron pills for candy.)

SCIENTISTS AND GOVERNMENTS AROUND

the world began cooperating in the Human Genome Project, a $3 billion, 15-year research effort to compile an international genetic data bank. Citing ethical questions about gathering and centralizing people's genetic data in huge computers, Dr. Paul Billings, chief of genetic medicine at the California Pacific Medical Center, indicated that genetic data banks are already proliferating. "The FBI is collecting genetic information," he said. "The insurance industry has large computer banks. The Army is collecting a DNA sample from every recruit. This will soon back up the largest genetic data bank in the world."

IN A CAMPAIGN TO PURGE THE GOVERN-

ment of homosexual civil servants, Canadian police in the 1960s tested a machine developed to identify gays. According to documents obtained in 1992 under Canada's Access to Information Act, the device, known as the "fruit machine," was a box that measured pupil size, palm sweat, and blood flow while displaying sexually provocative pictures. Although the machine was tested, the program was abandoned as unworkable. The documents showed that from 1959 to 1967, police opened files on 8,200 known or suspected gay men in Ottawa, hundreds of whom were purged.

DETAILS MAGAZINE REPORTED THAT

among the latest devices employers are using to keep track of workers' productivity are: an identification card with the bearer's fingerprint encoded on a magnetic strip that can reveal how many times the worker used the rest room; a toilet stall that automatically checks for drugs in the urine; toilet doors that open after a set time, regardless of whether the user is finished.

SCIENTISTS AT MICHIGAN STATE UNIV-

ersity and Virginia's James Madison University announced that they succeeded in genetically engineering a plant to produce biodegradable polyester. A statement from Michigan State pointed out that the plant plastic costs about $12 a pound, whereas permanent polyester made from oil costs only about 50 cents a pound.

CHRYSLER CORPORATION REQUESTED

that 380 workers who wash, wipe, and prepare Jeep Cherokees and Comanches for painting stop using antiperspirant deodorant. The company explained that falling flakes from antiperspirants contain chemicals, such as zinc zirconium, that can blemish the paint on the sport utility vehicles by causing "craters." Chrysler said that workers weren't banned from wearing antiperspirants, just "being educated about the problem," although spokesperson Scott Fosgard acknowledged that one woman filed a grievance after her supervisor asked to check her armpits.

IN THE FIRST OFFICIAL STEP TOWARD recognizing compulsive gambling as an illness, doctors in Spain conducted a series of successful trials by giving gambling addicts the drug fluvoxamine. The antidepressant, which is thought to cure people who suffer from obsessive compulsive disorders, such as the need to repeatedly wash their hands or count lampposts, appears to increase the serotonin levels, taking away the compulsive desire to bet.

ROBOTS TO THE RESCUE

• Japan's agriculture ministry announced plans to develop robot farm workers to take the place of the millions of humans abandoning the land for jobs in cities. A ministry official noted that the number of farmers had dropped from 6 million in 1960 to 3.8 million in 1991, and 30 percent of the farmers remaining are 65 or older.
• Robots may also serve in armies as early as next century, doing much of the dirty work of war that is now done by human soldiers, according to a study of future military technologies. A team of 100 experts assembled for the National Academy of Sciences predicted that by 2020, millions of computers will be used on the battlefield to collect information and robots will do the dangerous tasks of spying, identifying hostile forces, clearing land mines, evacuating

the wounded, and fighting on the front lines. Fewer human warriors could mean increased chances of war, however, the study concluded, observing, "The publics of advanced nations may find war more acceptable if the number of casualties can be kept low."

• McDonald's applied for a patent for "a food preparation device that can be operated by a robot." Developed at McDonald's Oak Brook, Illinois, research facility, the robot moves on tracks between the grill, griddle, and frying pan. Its arms can grab raw hamburgers, slap them on the grill, then grab hamburger buns and warm them, while cooking french fries. When the robot determines that the food is ready, it dumps everything in a holding bay for the human staff to deliver to customers. McDonald's said the fully automated cooking system will reduce labor costs and the amount of unsold cooked food that has to be thrown away. Although the first robots are already available, inventor John Reinertsen explained that it's still cheaper to employ humans than to install the robot.

SCIENTISTS FROM WOODS HOLE OCEAN-

ographic Institution in Massachusetts proposed getting rid of sewage sludge, the by-product of human waste from sewer systems after it has been treated, by dumping it on the ocean floor at least 300 miles offshore. They theorize that the sludge would stay put because deep-sea currents move so slowly. Hoping to test their theory, the center's scientists said they wanted funding to lower 1 million tons of sewage sludge through 16,000 feet of water on hoists with leak-proof buckets the size of houses, then dump it on the floor of the Atlantic between the East Coast and Bermuda. "No matter how much we recycle and conserve and reduce waste, we're still going to have some," said Charles D. Hollister, a marine geologist and senior scientist at Woods Hole. "Does it make sense to close off 70 percent of the Earth's surface without at least studying the idea of using it for waste disposal?"

A GOVERNMENT SCIENTIST IN WALES AN-
nounced that he has cracked the genetic code of four-leaf clovers and would start growing them to sell.

GREG JEFFREYS, AN AUSTRALIAN VEGE-
table farmer, invented a way to kill cockroaches without using chemical pesticides. His patented device uses fresh bait to lure the roaches to an electronic trap that unleashes a lethal 6,000-volt charge. A university test verified the zapper's effectiveness, noting that it reduced the roach population by 90 percent in six days.

RESIDENTS OF 13 HOMES IN A NEW SUB-
division in Oakley, California, reported that something in their water was causing stomach cramps, diarrhea, and fluorescent-colored stools. Authorities advised people in the Fairhaven Parc development of 91 homes to drink bottled or filtered water while they investigated. County health specialist Bill Grossi admitted he was stumped by the complaints of glowing stools.

THREE CZECHS WHO TRIED TO QUIT SMOK-
ing by using carrots as a substitute for cigarettes ate so many that their skin turned orange, according to psychiatrists Dr. Ludek Cerny and Dr. Karel Cerny, who noted

that when supplies of carrots ran low their patients "lapsed into heightened irritability." One patient, a 40-year-old man, who turned to carrots when he stopped smoking, was "soon eating carrots constantly, consuming up to five bunches a day," the psychiatrists reported in the *Journal of Addiction*, causing them to speculate that carrots may contain an "active substance conducive to drug addiction."

IN COLOMBIA, WHICH GROWS SOME OF the world's best coffee, the Federation of Coffee Producers created the Center for the Preparation of Coffee to teach Colombians to brew a decent cup of coffee, the newspaper *El Espectador* reported, because so few know how.

TAIWAN ANNOUNCED THE LAUNCHING OF a $2.5-million promotional campaign to persuade citizens to eat more rice. Worried that rising consumption of Western-style fast food is making people fat and undermining traditional Chinese culture, the cabinet's Council of Agriculture led off the campaign by reminding citizens that 5,000 years of growing and eating rice has instilled the virtues of hard work and thrift in Chinese people.

THE JAPANESE DEVELOPED "ANTI-NAP Man" for truck drivers, train engineers, students, and others who need to stay awake. The device consists of a sensor ring worn on the index finger. If the finger goes a certain amount of time without moving, the sensor triggers an alarm, which can hit 105 decibels.

COWABUNGA, DUDE

• To save scarce landfill space, some North Carolina farmers began feeding their cattle waste cotton from textile mills. Harriet & Henderson Yarns Inc., pointing out that it disposes of some 30 tons a week of raw cotton fibers too short for processing, crushed stalks, seeds, and dust, asked the state Cooperative Extension Service in Vance County to help find a way to dispose of it. Livestock agent Ben E. Chase suggested the feeding program to farmers. "They thought I was crazy," he said, "but now they report the cows love it."

• Kansas began testing a bus that runs on cows. Kansas Agriculture Secretary Sam Brownback predicted that the so-called biodiesel fuel, which is about 30 percent beef tallow and 70 percent diesel, would reduce pollution and create a market for beef fat.

• Researchers at Japan's Prefectural Animal Husbandry Experiment Station announced they were teaching cattle to respond to the beep of pocket pagers hung around the animals' necks so they will head for their feeding station with just a phone call instead of having to be rounded up.

• A Dutch company, Prolion, announced development of a robot that can milk cows without the farmer needing to attach the machine to their teats and detach them when the milking is done. The milking robot system uses ultrasound beams to locate the udder and teats. The company explained the system will save time and increase productivity 10 to 20 percent because cows can be milked more often.

• American researchers are taking a different approach to finding the teats. According to Walt Williams, who heads the research at the University of Maryland's Agricultural Experiment Station, they program their prototype robot milking machine with the position of the teats on each cow. Because udder shape and teat location change as the udder fills with milk, the researchers measured the location of cows' teats every four hours during lactation, then used the data to develop a computer model so the robot can calculate the location of a cow's teats on its own.

The Maryland researchers also uncovered evidence that, contrary to conventional wisdom, feeding may not be the reason cows return to their stalls to be milked. The robot-milked cows come even when no food is offered, according to Mark Varner, who is studying the cows' behavior. "They may just like to be milked," he said, adding that the scientists have trouble getting the cows to leave the milker even after they've been milked.

PANASONIC INTRODUCED AN ELECTRONIC

combination toilet seat and bidet that uses a warm-water spray and gentle drying, which company spokesperson Bob Falzone said "will set the standard in toilet systems of the future." Named IntiMist, it was priced at $1,199.

According to the company's press release: "Users activate the unit by sitting. Two self-cleaning water nozzles, precisely directed to the proper areas of the body, are controlled by buttons on an easily accessible side panel. Water pressure and temperature, air temperature and seat temperature can all be adjusted to suit individual preference. When the seat is vacated, all functions shut off automatically."

RICHARD R. WOOTEN, 37, OF BOWIE,

Maryland, invented a device that lets dogs use a home's toilet when they have to go. Designed for small dogs whose owners don't like walking them, the lightweight contraption wheels into place over a regular toilet. It has a platform that swings down to be washed with a jet spray after the dog leaves. He said that he plans to sell the Walk-Me-Not for $300.

Wooten, who's allergic to dogs and whose living room walls display large, framed photographs of small dogs using his invention, said he got his inspiration while stationed in Paris where everyone has a dog and "there's so much stuff on the ground you can't walk straight." He spent eight years developing the puppy potty, sacrificing a normal life. "I'd like to have a family, have kids, but I don't need the responsibility because I have to do things (for the Walk-Me-Not) at a moment's notice," he said. "I don't want to say 'I can't go to this meeting because I have to take my son to the baseball game.'"

IN AUBURN, WASHINGTON, KAREN

Bencze said her 10-year-old son used the Heimlich maneuver to save his choking 8-year-old brother. Bencze explained that the older boy learned the lifesaving technique by watching the animated television show "The Simpsons."

SCIENTISTS SEEKING NEW WAYS TO END

world hunger announced development of a goo-oozing hairy potato that fights pests without using the high doses of insecticides now needed to protect potato crops. According to K. V. Raman, a scientist at the International Potato Center in Lima, Peru, the hairs on the new potato plant's stalks and leaves secrete a sticky substance that traps and kills small insects as they feed or reproduce. The same sticky secretion strikes any larger Colorado beetle that eats the leaves with a serious case of constipation, which causes its stomach to bloat, crushing its ovaries, and curtailing reproduction.

AUTHORITIES INVESTIGATING WHY HART-
ford, Connecticut, residents were excluded from federal grand juries for three years discovered that a computer had listed everybody in the city as dead. Officials explained that the city's name had been listed in the wrong place on computer records, forcing the "d" at the end of "Hartford" into the column used for information about jurors. Whenever a resident's name popped up, the computer noted the "d," which stands for death, and a juror questionnaire was not sent.

THE GOVERNMENT DISCLOSED IT IS
spending $200,000 to figure out how to warn future generations of buried nuclear waste. The Department of Energy will seal 300,000 barrels of plutonium-contaminated byproducts from nuclear weapons factories inside salt caverns near Carlsbad, New Mexico. Although the drums will be 2,000 feet below the surface, they will remain dangerously radioactive for the next 10,000 years. Officials worry that during that time someone might accidentally drill into the site, causing a nuclear catastrophe. Thirteen experts have proposed warning signs, including menacing stone monoliths or earthworks to repel those tempted to tamper with the sealed entrance shaft, 70-foot concrete spikes, a field of sharp pyramids, and a sprawling map of Earth, with stone spikes marking the hazardous sites.

Some of the experts rejected the idea of sinister earthworks. "It would be a mistake to try and scare future people," said anthropologist David Givens, "because in the past that hasn't paid off."

ODE DE COLOGNE

• University of Colorado scientists cloned sweat collected from the armpits of country singer Sammy Kershaw to produce a cologne for the New York company Starclone, whose ads touted it as "an expression of the sharing nature of country music. A fragrance inspired by Sammy's songs." Paul Fennessey, a Colorado professor of pediatrics and pharmacology, explained that he obtained Kershaw's sweat from four star-shaped cotton pads sewn into the armpits of his shirt during a concert performance. Starclone, meanwhile, reportedly began lining up other entertainers and sports figures to turn their sweat into cologne.

• Other University of Colorado scientists developed a "bee perfume" that they said could be used to tame highly aggressive "killer" bees invading the United States, the British journal *Nature* reported. According to Michael D. Breed and Glennis E. Julian, the hive would accept a European queen bee treated with the scent as a replacement for their own queen, breeding with her and thereby genetically reducing the African bees' aggressiveness.

• When a scent manufactured by a Chicago company was spread around slot machines in the Las Vegas Hilton, the amount of money gambled at the machines increased an average of 45 percent. Alan Hirsch, a neurologist and psychiatrist who conducted the experiment, predicted, "It is quite possible that, within the next few years, the use of odorants as a gambling incentive will be as common as neon lights in the streets of Las Vegas."

Hirsch, founder of the Smell and Taste Treatment and Research Foundation, also reported that one of Detroit's Big Three automakers hired him to develop a scent that when sprayed on car salespeople will make them smell honest.

• Seafirst Bank, which has 285 branches in Washington State, started applying fragrances to money in its automatic teller machines. The bank said it hoped to make customers think its money is better than money dispensed by its competitors.

• Charles Wysocki, a smell researcher at the Monell Chemical Senses Center in Philadelphia, reported that several companies in England and Australia have begun using androstenone to make customers pay their bills promptly. Androstenone is a volatile steroid found in underarm sweat and urine in humans, and male pigs emit it to prompt females to mate. "For people who get a bill in the mail and it stinks like human urine," Wysocki said, "I can see why they would want to get it the hell out of the house."

HORMONE PILLS, TAKEN BY A WOMAN TO
rid herself of excess facial hair, also made her pet rottweiler sexually obsessed with her. Writing in the British medical journal *The Lancet*, Leeds dermatologist John Cotterill said that the pills may have subtly changed the woman's body odor, so that the dog "would not leave her alone." The woman solved her problem by having the dog castrated.

ISRAELI ARMY RESEARCHERS AN-
nounced they were working to develop a "salt bullet" to use against Palestinian stone throwers. "To an observer they look more like a package of candies or heartburn tablets,"

the army magazine *Bemahane* reported, "but those who know hope these bullets will act as a deterrent because, as opposed to rubber and sand bullets, they are intended to cause burning on the skin that will pass only after a day or two."

THREE ENGINEERS NEAR ALBUQUERQUE,

New Mexico, patented an isolation booth where smokers can satisfy their cravings without bothering nonsmokers who are in the same room. Resembling a telephone booth, the free-standing "smoker's booth" is open in front and features clear plastic sides that shield the top half of a person's body. The ceiling, similar to a self-contained stove hood, features fans that pull air through filters that trap the smoke and smell, then release the purified air back into the room.

A BROTHER-SISTER TEAM IN POCASSET,

Massachusetts, patented a capsule that lets people fend off attackers by spitting citric acid in their eyes. Made with wax and filled with concentrated citric acid, the capsule is designed to be tucked behind a person's cheek until it is needed. If an assault occurs, the victim bites into the capsule to release the citric acid, then spits it into the assailant's eyes.

CATHEDRALS IN TURIN, PISA, LUCCA, AND

other Italian cities installed air-conditioned confessional boxes. The confessionals, each costing $10,000, also include heating, soundproofing, and soft lighting.

LEON G. SCHUMACHER, AN AGRICUL-
tural engineer from the University of Missouri at Columbia, devised a pickup truck that runs on a mixture of 70 percent diesel fuel and 30 percent soybean oil. Schumacher said that although his alternative fuel burns cleaner and stretches mileage by as much as 25 percent a gallon, soybean oil tends to congeal at 30 degrees or colder. He added that another characteristic of the fuel mixture is "it smells like french fries."

THE 1992 UNITED NATIONS CONFERENCE
on Environment and Development in Rio de Janeiro caused a serious pollution problem. Brazilian scientists and environmentalists reported that the influx of 30,000 attendees left the area around the Riocentro conference site mired in sewage after overtaxing local treatment facilities. Fernando Almeida, a scientist at Rio's Federal University, calculated that the 12-day Earth Summit added nearly 13,000 gallons of barely-treated sewage to nearby streams and rivers, killing thousands of fish and boosting pollution levels on beaches nearly six miles away.

IN BAYVIEW, IDAHO, DAVID P. MURRAY RE-
ceived a patent for an artificial lake that soaks up pollutants carried in runoff from streets and lawns. The lake is a breeding tank for many aquatic plants that can cleanse water by absorbing chemical pollutants. Murray dismissed the conventional wisdom of lake developers—that such plants are weeds that should be killed—by explaining that his lake is designed to foster their growth and to make it easy to trim them back as if they were a lawn being mowed.

RESEARCHERS AT STANFORD UNIVERSITY

found and cloned a gene from bacteria that manufacture natural fertilizer on the roots of certain legume plants such as peas, beans, alfalfa, and clover. "The pipe-dream fantasy is that we could get non-legumes like wheat, corn, and barley to do this, too," said Robert F. Fisher, one of the Stanford scientists. "That would turn the whole game of agriculture around. Farmers wouldn't have to use industrial fertilizers."

WITHIN WEEKS OF THE ANNOUNCEMENT

that a fully biodegradable plastic had been developed from plant resins to replace the polyethylene container and would be used to bottle a new line of shampoo, Frederick F. Shih, a chemist at the Agricultural Research Service's center in New Orleans, reported that he was developing soybean plastics for use as an environmentally acceptable alternative to the plastic film widely used to protect food. The protein extracted from ground soybeans can be cast into a thin, dry sheet that retards spoilage or, since the coating is edible, food can be dipped directly into a solution of the stuff.

PATENT—AND JUDGMENT— PENDING

The Chinese military has invented the "dagger gun." The gun fires four bullets. When the ammo runs out, a dagger flips out from the handle. The gun also features a saw, scissors, a file, and can and bottle openers.

THE UNIVERSITY OF CALIFORNIA AT SAN

Francisco developed the Active Compression-Depression Resuscitator, which features a rubber suction cup attached to a horizontal handle. The device, which tests showed draws far more air into a victim's lungs than standard CPR, was inspired by an incident in which a heart-attack victim was revived by pumping his chest with a toilet plunger.

THE SAFE SEX SOFA WAS INTRODUCED AT

the Pacific Design Center's Wild West Week annual design fair in 1992. It consists of a flower-shaped chair and a chaise lounge and features taped messages promoting safe sex that play whenever anyone sits down.

XYTRONYX INC. DEVELOPED TANNING

patches for those worried about the dosage of ultraviolet rays they receive while out in the sunlight. Called Sun Alert, the badge is a plastic circle with an adhesive backing to attach to clothes or skin. The patch is blue but turns green and then yellow as it is exposed to more and more ultraviolet radiation. When it turns orange, people are alerted that they will get a sunburn.

MATSUSHITA ELECTRIC INDUSTRIAL COM-

pany invented a 36-square-foot wool carpet that features both heat and built-in stereo speakers. The carpet is wired to heat up like an electric blanket, and it has four thin speakers in its four corners. After attaching it to a CD player or other sound source, the user adjusts a control box to adjust volume as well as temperature.

THE FRENCH COMPANY PERIGOT HAD TO

order a recall of its popular Rigaud candles in 1990 after receiving reports that they "blew up like blowtorches." Although available in six scents, apparently only the cypress-scented green and cinnamon-scented rose candles were affected. The company referred to the defect as a "combustion problem."

WHEN JAPANESE VIDEO GAMES ARE

translated for use in the American market they often have to be redrawn to rid them of sexist and racist stereotypes that would offend most Americans. In its Japanese version, the "Final Fight" game features a hero hitting and head-butting a number of curvaceous female villains, who are replaced by male punks in the American version.

In "Joe & Mac," four cavemen enter a cave to the sound of women screaming and the cave shaking suggestively, only to emerge dragging the women by their hair. The scene is completely removed from the U.S. version. In "D.J. Boy," the hero fights an obese black woman in both versions of the game, only in the Japanese version she periodically makes a farting sound. Its maker, Kanejo USA, said that Japanese programmers of the U.S. version "were looking for input, and obviously they got it from the wrong people."

IN 1992 THE NORTH AMERICAN AIR DE-

fense Command disclosed that it was tracking about 7,000 spacecraft and debris larger than a square yard currently in orbit around the Earth. Industry consultant Walter L. Morgan said that with the demand for more satellite communications rising, "finding desirable, empty orbit locations for these new satellites will not be easy." The Federal Communications Commission tried to help by ruling that orbiting communications satellites no longer had to be 4 or 5 degrees apart but needed only 2 degrees of separation (about 914 miles).

When older satellites are retired or begin to break down, they are jettisoned into much higher "graveyard" orbits since attempts to destroy them might result in shattering them into thousands of pieces of debris that would further crowd orbiting space and endanger other satellites and spacecraft. When a 5-ounce projectile traveling at more than 2,000 miles a minute hit the Navy's 120-pound Oscar satellite in one experiment, Oscar broke into an estimated 30 million pieces.

SUBMITTED FOR YOUR CONSIDERATION: DON'T PANIC!

• Thieves in Kyrgyzstan, a Central Asian republic formerly part of the Soviet Union, stole 500 pounds of potassium cyanide from a factory there. The poison causes dizziness, convulsions, collapse, and assures an agonizing death. *Tass* said that the amount stolen was enough to poison "virtually the whole population of the Commonwealth of Independent States. If it is in the hands of criminal elements, we can expect the very worst."

• U.S. intelligence sources suggested that three tactical nuclear weapons reported missing from an arsenal in Kazakhstan had been sold to Iran. Months later Russian General Viktor Samoilov reportedly gave a briefing in the Ukraine in which he disclosed that three more nuclear warheads, designed for use on strategic missiles, had disappeared from

a storage facility somewhere in the former Soviet Union.
• Only days apart in June 1992, police in Romania reported
the theft of uranium from a nuclear facility while Austrian
police seized uranium believed stolen from the former
Czechoslovakia. In 1991 a Romanian technician had been arrested for stealing 460 pounds of tablets containing uranium.
• Romano Dolce, an Italian prosecutor in Como, said that
supplies of Soviet uranium and plutonium were being offered for sale abroad, "destined for countries using East
Bloc technology such as Iraq and Libya." In one arrest of a
Swiss businessman caught peddling plutonium, Dolce said
that documentary evidence was found concerning the sale
of nuclear artillery shells stolen from a base in Irkutsk.
• The German newspaper *Welt am Sonntag* reported in late
1992 that nuclear scientists from the former Soviet Union
were hard at work in various Third World countries. The
paper, quoting a report to the country's Cabinet by the
BND intelligence service, said that 50 of the scientists were
working in Iraq, including a laser specialist and a Ukrainian
expert on multiple warheads.

TAKAHIRO KOBAYASHI, SPOKESMAN FOR

the Tadano Corp., said that the Japanese construction crane
producer was sending a team to Easter Island to study the
mysterious stone head statues there and design a plan to
right those that have fallen. The statues weigh more than
50 tons and range from 16 to 33 feet tall. The company donated $1.5 million toward the restoration project, which was
approved by the government of Chile, owner of Easter Island. "There will ultimately be a chemical finish provided to
the stones to prevent further salt erosion," said Hiroyuki
Takagi, a member of the restoration committee.

CHINESE AUTHORITIES APPROVED THE

plan of Chinese civil engineer Cao Shizhong, 61, to straighten the Leaning Tower of Pisa to the degree of tilt it had in 1350. The tower leans 16.5 feet from the perpendicular, and experts fear its imminent collapse. Cao, who reportedly dreamt of the project for 20 years, said it would take 10 months to accomplish. He is known for righting a listing Ming dynasty pagoda in Zhejiang province.

MEXICO CITY MAYOR MANUEL CAMACHO

Solis announced that the city was considering fighting air pollution by using giant fans. Pollution in Mexico City is so severe that the city often experiences air-quality emergencies in which schoolchildren must be kept indoors, government cars are kept off streets, and factories are forced to reduce operations. The idea was proposed by engineer Herbert Castillo, head of the city's branch of the leftist Democratic Revolutionary Party. He suggested installing 100 wind machines, each 150 feet in diameter, around the city to shoot heated air into the sky whenever smog readings rise above the safe level, to drive holes into the surrounding air pressure zone that holds pollution inside the volcanic basin containing Mexico City and its suburbs.

Previous suggestions to rid Mexico City of its smog included drilling large holes in the surrounding mountains so that the smog would pass through them, adding perfume to car exhaust, and simply giving everyone a gas mask. Air quality there has deteriorated so badly that the country's Health Ministry predicts pollution-related deaths could soon reach 5,000 a year. Dr. Daniel Aguilar, an immunologist and a specialist in children's allergies, commented, "We advise parents to take their children and leave the city. Permanently."

GOOD AS NEW!

A youth group cleaning graffiti wiped away part of a 15,000-year-old painting of a prehistoric bison in the Mayrieres Cave near Brunquiel in southwest France. "Absolutely stupid!" said Rene Gachet, director of cultural affairs for the department of Tarn-et-Garonne.

Carlo T. E. Gay, writing of the preceding incident in a letter to *The New York Times*, noted that he could attest to the erasure of "three priceless line drawings of the Olmec culture—a figure and two animal heads, dating from 1000 to 500 B.C." in the Juxtlahuaca Cave, State of Guerrero, Mexico. Gay had dated the drawings himself while on visits there in the 1960s, only to return 23 years later to find that someone had rubbed them "with an abrasive agent or instrument."

CALLING DR. BENWAY!
CALLING DR. BENWAY!

Convinced that her breast implants were causing her immune system to go awry, Laura Thorpe, 39, used a blade from a disposable razor to cut open her left breast and remove the silicone gel herself. Thorpe, who lives in a mobile home near Bloomfield, Arizona, said her insurance company refused to pay for the operation because the implants were listed as cosmetic and doctors told her the operation would cost $5,000, which she didn't have. She explained that she learned how to perform the operation by visiting a doctor in Albuquerque, who described the procedure for her. "I just listened and went home and did it myself," she said, explaining that she waited until her husband and three children had gone to bed, then made the incision by following previous incision lines. "My thinking was that 100 percent I'm going to die and if I do it I have a 50–50 chance of maybe living," she said, "and I'll take that over dying."

Doctors at an Austin, Texas, hospital were forced to remove the silicone breast implants from Marlene Hooker, 46, after she repeatedly slashed her left breast with a scalpel. Hooker said that she had sought removal of the implants after being diagnosed with autoimmune disease, but her insurance company refused to pay.

U.S. SURGEON GENERAL ANTONIA NO-

vello blasted the makers of Crazy Horse malt liquor in 1992 as being "insensitive to the plight of the American Indian and the progress that has been made against alcohol abuse on reservations." Novello said that Crazy Horse was marketing itself to "yuppies" who had seen the film *Dances With Wolves*. Hank Shafran, spokesman for Hornell Brewing Co., the distributor of Crazy Horse, said that the company looked at the product "as celebrating a great Native American, not denigrating him."

The U.S. Bureau of Alcohol, Tobacco and Firearms notified the importer of Black Death Vodka in 1992 that the drink's marketing and the smiling skull logo on its label were deemed misleading and illegal. The company's marketeer, Black Death U.S.A., caused an uproar when it announced an endorsement deal with guitarist Slash from the rock group Guns N' Roses. The company said that it was targeting the 21 to 33 age group who are rock fans and said that "we didn't pick [Slash] because he has a hell-raising image." Black Death comes packaged in small black coffins.

RADIATION SPREAD FURTHER FROM THE

damaged nuclear reactor at Chernobyl when wildfires caused by dry weather burned grass and brush in the area, sending radioactive ash flying. Without giving details as to the geographic spread of the radiation, the *Itar-Tass* news agency noted that the fires burned particularly fiercely in the villages surrounding the reactor site that have been abandoned since the disaster.

LIFE MAGAZINE INTERVIEWED 100 TOP EX-

perts on aging, many of whom said that life spans would eventually last centuries given their expectations that "a manageable number of human genes" controlling the aging process will be manipulated in coming years. Although most researchers were modest in their forecasts, Dr. Michael Jazwinski of the Louisiana State University Medical Center predicted, "Some people alive now may still be alive 400 years from now."

EVEN THOUGH DOCTORS SAID THAT 18-

month-old Heaven Leigh Yarbrough, born with cerebral palsy, would never walk, after watching Billy Ray Cyrus's "Achy Breaky Heart" music video on television, she took her first steps. When her mother, Marjorie Yarbrough, bought the video to play it again, "Heaven stood up, walked into the living room, then outside and down the sidewalk."

She added: "[Now] anytime his music comes on, she stops what she's doing and starts dancing around and singing."

ACCORDING TO A STUDY OF "SLEEP-

Related Eating Disorders" in the journal *Sleep*, sufferers demonstrated a variety of eating-while-asleep behavior ranging from eating small snacks to preparing large meals. Because they were asleep, "impaired judgment and sloppiness were common, as patients ate raw or cooked food with their hands, poured food on themselves, attempted to drink ammonia cleaning solution, dropped food on the floor, or took items out of the freezer and scattered them around the house. They also indiscriminately put large quantities of sugar or salt on food, and ate butter and sugar by the spoonful." Many were scalded by the "impulsive consumption of very hot beverages or oatmeal." Several hurt themselves by bumping into furniture and walls during "frenzied running to the kitchen."

Nature Runs Amok

APPLE COMPUTERS APPOINTED A GORILLA
that speaks sign language to the advisory board of a program studying the nature of intelligence. To allow Koko to take part in meetings, the company created a special computer to give her an audible voice.

PRO PRIMATES, A DUTCH ANIMAL RIGHTS
group founded by Ignaas Spruit, formed the world's first trade union for monkeys. The group said it hopes to negotiate better living conditions, including arranging early retirements, for the 1,600 primates in Dutch labs and zoos.

BAD BUGS

• The Giant Tusked Weta, an insect discovered in 1989, sports tusks, can jump like a grasshopper, eats meat, and grows larger than a mouse. So far it has been found only on one very small island off New Zealand's North Island that holds only several hundred of them. Entomologist Mary MacIntyre said that the weta is a survivor of a prehistoric era, adding, "It's entirely fortuitous that these weird things have managed to survive at all."

• In 1990, mysterious diamond-shaped insects, each carrying 30 tiny stingers, attacked hundreds of people in Bangladesh, killing at least 30. The bug's bite kills within four hours. Villagers responded by burning the bushy, three-meter-tall, inedible plants that harbored the bugs.

• Large tropical grasshoppers that grow up to five inches long and have the wingspan of a small bird appeared in Florida in 1992. The giants are native to Trinidad, Costa Rica, and Venezuela. Harold Denmark of the Florida Department of Agriculture described the grasshopper as "monstrous looking," adding, "It looks like it's not for real. It is—and it does fly."

WILD IN THE STREETS

Hazel Murphey sued a Houston motel after the death of her husband in a Brazilian fire ant attack there. Murphey said that during a stay at the motel, the couple awoke to find hundreds of the thumbnail-sized ants crawling on their bed.

OFFICIALS IN BARTLETT, TEXAS, BLAMED

fire ants for the death of Minnie Gibson, 68, who died of smoke inhalation from a fire in her mobile home. The fire started when an army of fire ants from a colony in Gibson's yard swarmed into an electrical circuit-breaker box "and caused a short," explained Justice of the Peace Jimmy Bitz, noting, "The ants were just piled up in there."

A BUTTERFLY MIGRATION ESTIMATED AT

the billions swarmed through California's Sierra Nevada mountains in the summer of 1992, the largest since 1965. The orange, black, and white butterflies covered windshields and clogged car radiators on their journey northward. Dennis Murphy, director of Stanford University's Center for Conservation Biology, thinks the butterflies are an indicator of environmental change and believes that the migration, thought to be from 100 to 1,000 times its usual size, is an indicator that the state's drought may be easing.

TRUCK DRIVER JOHN PAUL SHANE, 43,

survived a crash that killed the driver of a car but then had to endure a three-hour rescue attempt while the millions of bees he had been transporting attacked him and his rescuers. Shane had been carrying 250 bee hives, each containing between 20,000 and 30,000 bees. Firefighters fought back, killing many of the bees with foam insecticide and spray.

WILLIAM BELNOSKE, 77, OF NEW WAVERLY,

Texas, apparently died of a heart attack after being stung more than 100 times by a swarm of attacking bees. Belnoske disturbed a hive of domesticated European bees while mowing his lawn.

A GROUP OF MONKEYS ENTERED THE

New Delhi office of India's Ministry of Urban Development through an open window and vandalized it, throwing files, and destroying rent bills. Officials said that the incident would result in weeks of delay in getting bills off to government-housing tenants.

A MOB OF AT LEAST 3,000 WILD HOGS,

some weighing as much as 400 pounds, were described as "out of control" at the 1,300-acre Seminole County, Florida, dump. The hogs tore up the dump's protective dirt layer to get at the rotting garbage, which was then left exposed. Since, according to federal law, if the county allowed the hogs to continue, it would be required to boil the garbage before the hogs ate it, the county hired a trapper at the rate of $22.50 per hog.

A LARGE 14-YEAR-OLD ORANGUTAN CON-

fronted a French tourist in a park on Borneo, grabbed him and undressed him, pulling off his pants, shirt, and underwear, according to a Malaysian official. Throughout the ordeal the tourist and his wife stood perfectly still. The orangutan then fled into the woods with the clothing.

FOLLOWING MASSIVE FLOODS, A DELUGE

of frogs invaded four villages in Iran's western highlands, covering farmland and disrupting highway traffic. Tehran Radio warned: "Millions of frogs have taken over the area."

AFTER TRYING FOR 40 YEARS TO WIN THE

Central Marking Race from France to England, Patrick Lees, 55, finally appeared to have won when his racing pigeon Billy Blue finished ahead of almost 1,000 other contestants in the 536-mile, 25-hour race. As the bird arrived at the finish line in Crookes, Sheffield, however, it was pounced upon and killed by a tomcat. Although Billy Blue was at least one-half hour ahead of his closest competition, by the time Lees retrieved the body and removed its leg ring to have it officially clocked in, two other birds had landed and Lees had to settle for third place.

LARGE NUMBERS OF RACING PIGEONS

mysteriously vanished during two separate races in 1992. In Australia on August 29, 8,100 pigeons were released from Hay, New South Wales, on a 340-mile race to Sydney. The race should have taken 6 hours but the first birds (80 in number) didn't arrive until the following day. By a week later, another 20 percent had arrived but the rest never showed up. "I have had 61 years of experience with racing pigeons and I have never seen anything like this before," said Sam Beggs, director of the Australian Pigeon Fanciers Association.

Then, on September 6, 99 pigeons competed in a race from Allegheny, New York, to West Haven, Connecticut. By two weeks later, only seven had shown up. Some theories about the disappearances have raised the possible effects of radar transmissions and other electromagnetic fields at work in the atmosphere and the possible effects they might all have on the birds' homing skills.

(Similar mysterious disappearances of racing pigeons were also reported in 1988 by pigeon clubs throughout Europe. Some West German clubs suspended racing for the rest of the season after experiencing several large losses.)

HOLMEN, WISCONSIN, WAS THE SITE OF A

bizarre accident as a queen bee was struck by a car. She apparently was leading a swarm across the street when her death caused the swarm to become disoriented. They instinctively refused to leave without her. The resulting chaos as more and more bees were run over caused a 30-foot honey slick two to three inches deep with dead bees. A beekeeper noted that swarming bees first gorge on honey and then move to form a new colony. Despite a crowd watching the scene, no stings were reported.

IN DAVENPORT, WASHINGTON, A STRAY

white cat attacked Bonni Matheson while she did yard work, scratching and biting her hands. It then attacked her two sons, aged 18 and 15. Police Chief Jim Gants captured it with a skunk trap hours later. "It was the meanest cat I've ever seen," said Gants. "It would go right after you trying to get through the cage to get to you." Gants dropped the cat at the pound but it escaped two days into a 10-day rabies observation period. Once out, it returned to the Matheson house where Mrs. Matheson had just returned from the hospital after being treated for the first attack. Matheson said the cat "went right after us," entering the house where it destroyed the kitchen wallpaper and then attacked all three family dogs in the living room. After the family fled the scene, the cat was once again caged. Although it was determined to be rabies-free, it was destroyed.

IT'S GOT A GUN!!!

Police near Moscow found Gennady Danilov, 33, dead of a gunshot wound to the stomach. Next to the body was a gun and a dog whose hind legs had been caught in a trap. By studying the scratch marks found on the butt of the gun, police theorized that the dog first scratched off the gun's safety and then pulled the trigger.

IN MISSOURI, LARRY LANDS WAS SHOW-

ing off a turkey he had shot and put in his trunk when the not-yet-dead bird started thrashing around and pulled the trigger of Lands's gun, also in the trunk. Lands was shot in the leg. "The turkeys are fighting back," said county Sheriff Ron Skiles.

DON'T FOOL WITH MOTHER NATURE

A powerful storm uncovered the skull of a missing woman in New Jersey. "Without Mother Nature eroding the riverbank with a 100-year storm, we might not have found it," said Union County Prosecutor Andrew K. Ruotolo, Jr. After the skull was identified as that of Karen Sherrier, 31, of Brick Township, police arrested a man and charged him

with murder. Sherrier was last seen leaving a tavern with
him four months earlier.

SERIAL KILLER GIANT PANDAS ON THE LOOSE

After one year of study, China's senior panda experts still
were unable to explain why a renegade giant panda gave
up its natural diet of bamboo and went on a 10-month killing
spree in 1990, slaughtering at least 26 sheep. The panda was
captured and brought to the Wolong nature preserve in Si-
chuan Province. Reports surfaced later in 1992 that other
giant pandas had become carnivores. Officials blamed them
for killing and eating 48 sheep during the first half of the
year.

WE ARE IN CONTROL

A five-acre fire set in the Malheur National Wildlife Refuge
near Frenchglen, Oregon, as part of a wildlife study to test
a theory that worms and other invertebrates emerge earlier
in the year on burned land, went out of control, and burned
down 900 acres, destroying wetlands and bird habitats. A
refuge manager said that the flames jumped the fire line
and "just took off."

AFTER TANJA THE HIPPOPOTAMUS HAD

flattened 10 of her 15 babies, zookeepers in Amsterdam in-
jected the 30-year-old hippo with a contraceptive.

MRITHI, A 400-POUND MALE SILVER BACK

mountain ape who had appeared in the film *Gorillas in the Mist*, was found shot to death, an apparent victim of Rwanda's civil war. A fire fight between rebels and government troops had taken place in the area.

A 20-YEAR VETERAN OF THE TOWN COUN-

cil of Aalsmeer, near Amsterdam, charged with the responsibility of protecting the environment, confessed to the shooting of a heron, a protected bird. The man said that he shot the bird to stop it from eating the ornamental carp in his garden pond.

A MAN ILLEGALLY FISHING WITH EXPLO-

sives on Corsica was killed when a hand grenade he dropped exploded.

IN SEREMBAN, MALAYSIA, M. KRISHNAN,

45, was hospitalized with a stomach pain after he had become angry at a 12-inch snake that bit him and swallowed it whole.

MAUREEN NEIDHARDT, PUBLISHER OF EX-

otic Breeds Journal, reported that fainting goats are a "growing exotic pet trend, not a hot new fad." When startled, the animal's muscles stiffen and it falls over for 20 seconds to a full minute. Then it gets up. The goats weigh from 35 to 50 pounds and are 15 to 20 inches tall. "When I first got mine, just walking into the pen would make them faint," said Gail Degough of Gilroy, California. Ruth Prentice of the International Fainting Goat Association in Terrill, Iowa, said that there were 2,030 fainting goats registered in the United States in early 1992. Registration requires two photos taken from the goat's side and one taken just as it begins to fall over.

HOW GREEN IS MY DUNE BUGGY ATTACK SQUADRON?

According to reporting by Ivan Solotaroff in *Esquire*, in 1982 Charles Manson established Air, Trees, Water, Animals, an environmental organization run by his followers. In charge is former Manson Family member Sandra Good, who served 10 years for "threatening business and government leaders she felt were destroying the environment." Good lives just 25 miles from the imprisoned Manson. Commenting on the Tate-Lobianca murders, which she saw in terms of environmental politics, Good said, "What we did was necessary . . . to start a revolution against pollution! We made a statement and we wrote it in blood in the Tate house." Said Manson: "I seen the ocean dying up in Mendocino in '67. My water spirits are mad."

NOT DEAD YET

Eleven days after burying her dog Brandy, Patricia Corcoran of Botwood, Newfoundland, saw an announcement on television that someone had found a dog matching the description of the one she buried. "This may sound crazy," said

Corcoran, "but I just had the feeling it was Brandy." Indeed, it was. Corcoran theorized that although she thought Brandy's heart had stopped beating, it was just unconscious and was later able to dig out of the two-foot-deep grave. "The place was still covered with the exception of one small hole where I guess she was digging her way up and pushing some of the soil back down." Corcoran said that while she wasn't spooked by her dog's return from the grave, "a lot of people who've heard about it have been."

WARNING! WARNING!

On July 3, 1992, an 18-foot high, 27-mile-long rogue wave rose out of a calm sea and crashed ashore on Daytona Beach, Florida, injuring 75. The wave, coming out of water that was otherwise rising to only one or two feet at the time, sent people running as it pushed cars under the boardwalk, piled sailboats on top of cars, and damaged six blocks of boardwalk. Seismologists at first said that the wave was caused by an underwater landslide, but days later changed their minds and suggested that thunderstorms over the Atlantic churned up the ocean and caused the wave. Mark Albertelly of the National Weather Service said that weather buoys offshore never registered anything unusual prior to the wave's appearance. Volusia County chief beach ranger John Kirvan said: "I've got men who've been here 30 years, and they've never seen anything like it."

MOACYR SCHROEDER, SUPERINTENDENT

of the Brazilian Institute of the Environment, said that more than 500 penguins were found dead on southern Brazilian beaches in September 1991. They had traveled almost 1,860 miles from Patagonia and were diagnosed as having died from hunger and exhaustion. Schroeder said that he had no idea why they would have made such a trip.

IN 1987, UNIVERSITY OF ILLINOIS PLANT

explorer D. D. Soejarto discovered a tree in a Malaysian rain forest whose sap had yielded a compound that, when studied years later, had appeared to inhibit the growth of the AIDS virus. Soejarto returned to look for the tree in 1992, only to find that it had been cut down and used for construction.

ACCORDING TO RESEARCH BY LEADING

herpetologists, almost one-third of North America's 86 species of frogs and toads seem to be disappearing. While development and pesticides are blamed for some of the disappearances, no theory seems to account for all of them, most of which are occurring in wilderness areas. Said David B. Wake, director of the Museum of Vertebrate Zoology at the University of California at Berkeley, "I wish there were a death star to explain it. I don't see a single toxin, a single virus. My theory is that it's general environmental degradation. That's the worst thing. Frogs are telling us about the environment's overall health. They are the medium and the message."

Researchers on other continents have also seen a decline in frog populations. "Decline is very evident and very rapid in Europe," said Hansjurg Hotz of the University of Illinois. Others have reported declines of toads in Peru, frog species in Brazil, and salamanders in Mexico. However, some skeptical scientists doubt these claims, suggesting that

the evidence thus far tends to be anecdotal and that conclu-
sive data on frog populations will require rigorous study
over 10 to 20 years.

IT'S NOTHING, GO BACK TO BED

In June 1992, NASA's Hubble Telescope focused on a mas-
sive black hole in galaxy M51, 20 million light years away.
They had expected to see a black bar across the hole. What
they saw instead was a large dark "X" symbol across its
nucleus. "We have no idea what it is," said astronomer Ed
Weiler. "My joke is God wanted us to find a black hole so
he put a big X on it. This will send the theoreticians back
to their computers."

LOST IN THE OZONE

• University of California researchers suggested that one
way to repair the ozone hole that appears over Antarctica
each October would be having hundreds of large airplanes
release 50,000 tons of the hydrocarbons ethane and propane
into the antarctic stratosphere each year to soak up the pollutants that are attacking the ozone layer. "This is a concept
and not a proposal," said UC Irvine geoscientist Ralph Cic-
erone, who conceded that the action could inadvertently en-
large the ozone hole.
• Proposals to preserve the planet's ozone layer advanced at
the annual meeting of the American Geophysical Union in
1991 included lofting millions of small balloons into the stratosphere to reflect sunlight back into space; putting giant

umbrellas, each covering hundreds of square miles, in space to shade the planet; pouring 2 million tons of iron compounds into the Antarctic Ocean to cause a huge growth of plankton, enabling the ensuing biological frenzy to deplete the ocean's carbon dioxide and in turn soak up some of the excess from the atmosphere; and a Russian scheme to fire cannon shells full of chemicals into the stratosphere. F. Sherwood Rowland, an atmospheric chemist at UC Irvine, conceded, "Some of these ideas just slide right off the scale into science fiction."

• British scientists announced development of a hand-held sensor to warn people concerned about sunbathing in the ozone-depleted atmosphere how long they can safely remain exposed to the sun. The device can be adjusted to individual skin types.

• The Canadian government reported that more Canadians are developing cancer, particularly skin cancer caused by exposure to sunlight.

• As of September 1992, NASA measurements revealed that the Antarctic ozone hole was the largest on record, at that point covering an area three times larger than the United States. The Total Ozone Mapping Spectrometer instrument aboard the Nimbus-7 satellite showed that the ozone hole was 15 percent larger than when measured in 1991. A month later the Argentine weather service reported that the hole's outer edge had moved over Tierra del Fuego, a populated island off the southern tip of South America divided between Argentina and Chile.

• NASA also released data showing that the highest levels of ozone-destroying chemicals ever recorded had been detected over the Northern hemisphere. This was seen as an indication that a second ozone hole, this one over the Arctic, was imminent. "Everybody should be alarmed about this," said Michael J. Kurylo, manager of the upper atmosphere research program at NASA. "We're seeing conditions primed for ozone destruction. It's in a far worse way than we thought."

ACCORDING TO A REPORT IN THE BRITISH *Medical Journal,* Danish researchers found that men's average sperm count has nearly halved over the past 50 years and that semen quantity has decreased by almost 25 percent. They suggested that the drop may be due to environmental pollution.

THE SHAKIN', SHAKIN', SHAKES

A panel at the 1992 American Society of Civil Engineers' annual meeting in New York City said that the city had a 60 percent chance of suffering a major earthquake that would cause as much as $25 billion in damage. "You can expect in New York City an earthquake of a 5.0 magnitude roughly every 100 years," said Klaus Jacob, an engineer at Columbia University.

GEOLOGISTS REPORTED THAT THEY DIS-covered two previously unknown earthquake faults under downtown Los Angeles. The two faults pass under skyscrapers, along the Hollywood Freeway and near Dodger Stadium.

THE BIG ONE UPDATE

California installed the Earthquake Safety Hotline to answer nervous inquiries from folks across the state. The hotline gets about 50 to 60 calls a day, according to Hotline Agency spokesman Stef Donev, including one caller who wanted to know "if it was true they were putting pillars in Utah so when California fell off they would have a place to dock the boats carrying people going out to look for survivors."

DOOMSDAY 2126

The International Astronomical Union reported that comet Swift-Tuttle could strike the Earth on August 14, 2126. Previously seen during the Civil War, Swift-Tuttle was rediscovered in 1992. Astronomers now believe that it is responsible for the Perseids meteor shower each August as Earth passes through the debris it leaves in its wake. Swift-Tuttle is estimated to be about six miles in diameter, big enough to wreak havoc on the planet's climate and probably end civilization as we know it. Estimates are that its impact would be akin to having thousands of nuclear warheads exploding simultaneously on the same spot. "[There is] a small but non-negligible chance that [the comet] will hit" Earth, said Dr. Brian G. Marsden of the Harvard-Smithsonian Center for Astrophysics, who rated the risk of its impact at 1 in 10,000.

Later, Marsden revised his prediction, citing new evidence that suggests there is virtually no chance of Swift-

Tuttle hitting the Earth on its next pass. "We're safe for the next millennium," he said. "In the year 3044, we have the possibility of a very close approach." He refused to rule out the possibility of a direct hit at that time due to the inherent inaccuracies in making such long-term predictions.

JAPAN'S MINISTRY OF INTERNATIONAL

Trade and Industry reacted to an international trade ban on tortoise shells by announcing that it was spending $4 million to study the feasibility of a government-funded program to breed cockroaches to save the jobs of 1,500 craftsmen, who had been using the shells to fashion combs, jewelry, and frames for eyeglasses, by providing them with a new material.

IN CHINA'S JIANGXI PROVINCE, YANG SIGI,

a former exterminator suffering from snail fever, gastritis, and a neurotic disorder, cured himself after orthodox treatment failed by eating large quantities of termites for three months in 1987. Believing afterward that termites have a "magical medical power," he turned his interests to medicine and, according to New China News Agency, has opened three factories that make termite-based drugs to treat a variety of ills.

SCIENTISTS AT MICHIGAN TECHNOLOGI-

cal University reported finding a giant underground mushroom, weighing as much as 100 tons and covering 38 acres. Claiming it is the largest living thing on Earth, they noted that it is just one of many giant fungi around the world silently killing forests.

Less than one month later, scientists in Washington State announced they had found a fungus south of Mount Adams that is nearly 40 times bigger than the Michigan fungus. According to Ken Russell, a forest pathologist at the state Department of Natural Resources, the Washington fungus covers 1,500 acres.

RESEARCHERS AT THE OREGON GRADU-ate Institute, seeking ways to use organisms to clean up the environment, reported discovering that white rot fungus, common in forests throughout North America, Russia, and Scandinavia, thrives on cancer-causing PCBs and other toxic chemicals, turning them into harmless carbon dioxide and water.

LOUISIANA CRAWFISH, IMPORTED BY Spain 25 years ago to appeal to the national palate, today are devouring the country's rice fields. The regional government of Catalonia declared the mudbugs a plague in 1992 and instructed the Department of Agriculture to use all means to destroy them. Farmers tried gassing them, with no luck, and have begun using pesticides to eradicate the crawfish, which are twice the size of the native species, more resistant to pollution and, according to biologist Raul Escosa, "have a high reproductive level" and no predators. "I don't know exactly where Louisiana is," said rice farmer Juan Tiron, "but I wish the people there would come and take them back."

A HERD OF MIGRATING ELEPHANTS IN IN-

dia delayed their search for food by breaking into an Indian Army camp in West Bengal and stealing the soldiers' rum. According to the *New Delhi Statesman*, the elephants liked it so much that they keep coming back for more. The camp has tried electric fences and bonfires to keep the herd out, but the animals learned to use their trunks to hose out the fires and to demolish the fences with wooden logs. Once inside the camp, they break open the rum bottles, drink their fill, and stagger back into the forest.

IN INDIA'S EASTERN STATE OF ASSAM,

rampaging elephants killed at least 31 people in 1992 during attacks on villages. State wildlife Warden H. C. Changkakati explained that some of the attacks came after elephants seeking food broke into stores of rice beer.

NORWEGIAN AUTHORITIES HAD TO GAS

more than 1,000 rats that took over the house of an Oslo couple who had been breeding them to sell to a pet shop. The shop went bankrupt, police officer Klaus Henning Os explained, but the couple decided to keep a few unsold rats, including a pregnant female, who escaped from her cage. Soon the house was filled with rats roaming freely, gnawing the furniture, and forcing the couple to move out. "The man has personal problems and lost control," Os said. "Instead of seeking help, he started feeding the rats."

RATS CONTINUE TO PLAGUE BANGLA-

desh. The problem has gotten worse since the government began holding twice-yearly rat-killing campaigns and awarding prizes, such as color televisions, to whoever collects the most rat tails. Prize-minded contestants pour on powerful pesticides, which have scarcely dented the rat population but have all but destroyed snakes, owls, and other rat predators.

BESIDES HAVING TASTY, HIGH-PROTEIN,

low-fat meat, rats make healthful beverages. The *China Farmer's Daily* newspaper reported that processed "hairless rats" are a big seller for use in medicinal wines.

IN NEVADA, A HUNTERS' GROUP AN-

nounced that it would present $1,500 and its "conservationist of the year" award to hunters who turn in the most coyote carcasses.

Officials in the Australian state of Victoria announced that the government was offering prizes to hunters who turn in fox scalps. Foxes, brought to Australia in the 19th century and bred for hunting, now number 3 million and are killing off native species that they prey on. Under the eradication program, dubbed "Foxlotto," hunters receive lottery tickets good for resort holidays, dinners, and sporting goods.

OFFICIALS DISCLOSED THAT U.S. MILITARY

satellites are being used to track dung heaps in the Australian outback. Their reports help Australian researchers track the droppings of cattle, sheep, kangaroos, and goats to determine whether overgrazing in the sparse land is caused by farmers or nature.

AFTER YEARS OF ENCOURAGEMENT BY

conservationists, thousands of flamingos returned to a Spanish nature reserve to breed for the first time in centuries. Before their eggs could hatch, they were frightened away by firefighting aircraft that accidentally flew low over the restricted area scooping up water. "Within hours, the dozens of eggs left behind were attacked by gulls," said Alberto Martinez, director of the national park.

RESEARCHERS DISCOVERED A KIND OF

bacteria that is a million times larger than its one-celled cousins. The giant microbe, "Epulopiscium," was first observed in the intestines of a sturgeon in 1985 and has since been found in mice and guinea pigs. University of Indiana researcher Esther R. Angert said the single-cell behemoth was misidentified because no one thought bacteria could be so large. Norman R. Pace, the biology professor who directed the research project, said that scientists have no idea what function the giant bacteria perform but noted that it is more than "just a bunch of stuff floating around in a bag."

THE U.S. GEOLOGICAL SURVEY REPORTED

that scientists examining river muck discovered bacteria that can "eat" chlorofluorocarbons, which scientists say are the main threat to the ozone layer. Noting that the CFC-eating bacteria thrive only in oxygen-free environments, such as natural wetlands and man-made landfills, government microbiologist Derek Lovley said that they are harmless to humans.

MORE LIFE EXISTS INSIDE EARTH THAN ON
the surface, according to Cornell University astrophysicist Thomas Gold. Writing in *Proceedings of the National Academy of Science*, he explained that the teeming community of bacteria and microorganisms, much of it miles deep, draws its energy not from the sun but from the heat of Earth's core. Gold suggested that similar life forms may exist inside the Moon and other planets.

SWARMS OF PHANTOM ALGAE LURKING
in mud on the bottom of shallow coastal waters can burst forth from a state of suspended animation, swim into the water, release a poison that kills fish by the millions, feed on tissue from dying fish, then retreat into hiding, all within a matter of hours, according to researchers from North Carolina State University. The scientists blamed the one-celled microbes for at least nine major fish kills in North Carolina's Pamlico Sound and in nearby fish farms since May 1991.

CANADA, WHICH HAS 6 PERCENT MORE
land area than the United States but only one-tenth the population, claimed that it is running out of space in its landfills and has started sending its trash south of the border. A ruling by the U.S. government that lets Canadian trash cross the border without inspection, "because," officials said, "Canadians are just like us and so's their trash," has sent U.S. trash haulers north to earn fees for hauling away Canada's garbage.

WHEN STARKVILLE, MISSISSIPPI, FOUND

itself beset by as many as 7 million blackbirds, aldermen proposed solving the problem by hiring a plane to fly over the pine woods where the birds roost at night and spray them with liquid detergent. The lawmakers reasoned that when the next rain fell, the water would combine with the detergent to remove the oil from the birds' feathers, causing them to freeze to death.

JAPANESE FARMERS IN KISAKATA TRY-

ing to stop crows from damaging their rice and soybean crops began trapping 200 of the birds a month and eating them. The newspaper *Mainichi* quoted the mayor of the coastal town as saying, "They taste quite good."

U.S. DEPARTMENT OF AGRICULTURE IN-

spectors advised Carmen Shaw, who cares for sick and orphaned animals at her Back to Nature Wildlife Refuge in Bithlo, Florida, to get Judy, a 32-year-old 5-pound capuchin monkey, a television set or a VCR to "enrich her environment."

DEREK ALLEN, A FARMER IN RAMPISHAM,

England, reported that the tin roof of his pig sty acts as a radio receiver, picking up signals from a nearby British Broadcasting Corporation transmitter. Allen said the broadcasts in 36 languages and news bulletins "seem to soothe" the pigs, adding, "I'm sure my pigs know more about what's going on than I do."

6

Early Warning Signs
of Weirdness
We Now Know to Be Common

ON OCTOBER 3, 1978, ANTHONY HENRY of Dayton, Ohio, climbed over the White House fence and demanded to know why U.S. money bears the inscription "In God We Trust." An Associated Press photo of the incident shows Henry on the White House lawn, barefoot and dressed in a white karate uniform, holding a knife in his right hand and a book in his left. Shown raising the knife, he is surrounded by at least seven uniformed and plainclothes Secret Service officers, all wielding nightsticks. Two officers received minor knife wounds in the ensuing struggle.

IN 1968 RANDOLPH COUNTY, NORTH CAR-

olina, Sheriff Lloyd Brown announced that he was going to use bloodhounds to track the "vampires" on the loose throughout the county. The vampires were described as black animals, larger than foxes but with foxlike tails and long snouts. Brown said the vampires had killed hogs in two sections of Randolph 25 miles apart. They reportedly killed by sucking all the blood out of the victims, leaving the hogs otherwise undisturbed.

ON NOVEMBER 26, 1977, VIEWERS OF EN-

gland's Southern Television newscast heard a "spatial" voice interrupt the program and warn the people of Earth to destroy "all your weapons of evil." Hundreds of people panicked and called the station and police before the station announced that the interruption, which claimed to be "the voice of Glon, the voice of the Asteron Galactic Command," was a hoaxer who had succeeded in patching into a station relay transmitter.

BIG BEN STOPPED RUNNING FOR THREE

hours on December 15, 1989. Engineers blamed a mechanical problem. Days later psychic Uri Geller took responsibility, claiming that he was under contract with a U.S. firm that suggested he use his psychic power to stop Big Ben on New Year's Eve. Geller said that the December 15 stoppage was a dry run.

POLICE ARRESTED JOHNSON WATSON, 23,

in Clover Village, Indiana, in February 1977, for flinging sides of beef and his own clothing from a speeding truck on Interstate 74. A naked Watson was arrested after a foot chase through 8 to 10 inches of snow. He told police that he was "feeding the people."

IN NOVEMBER 1988, THE 300-FOOT RADIO

telescope at Green Bank, West Virginia, mysteriously collapsed into a pile of twisted metal girders. Built in 1963, the telescope, operated by the National Radio Astronomy Observatory, was regarded as one of the most powerful of its kind in the world. The collapse came one night with no warning while the device was in operation. "There was no wind, the weather was fine, and operation was normal up to the moment of the collapse," said Dr. George Seielstad, assistant director of the observatory. "At this point we have no idea what may have caused the accident."

Updates

MORE CODED MESSAGES

Former Beiruit hostage Edward A. Tracy, an American suspected of spying in Lebanon and held by Moslem fundamentalists for five years, held a news conference at which he identified his captors as members of a motorcycle club called "The Risk-Takers," of which he claimed he was once a member. Tracy said he was abducted in Beiruit over a dispute with a bookseller involving $10. At the time of the conference Tracy was still a patient in the psychiatric ward of the Veterans Administration Medical Center in Boston, where he was sent after his release.

666 News

An item in *New Scientist* noted that Universal Product Codes (bar codes) contain three "delimiters" to identify the product and the manufacturer. The "delimiters" are two thin stripes, which happen to represent the number six. This means that three sixes used in that manner appear on each and every bar code.

IN ARIZONA, THE YAVAPAI COUNTY BOARD
of Supervisors voted to change the name of a street in a Sedona subdivision from Satan's Arch Drive after 22 residents complained that the name was scaring away potential buyers. Named for a nearby rock formation, the street was renamed Arch Drive.

WHEN THE COMPUTER THAT ASSIGNS
drivers' license numbers in Anchorage, Alaska, began issuing the prefix 666, several drivers complained. "One lady said it was the mark of the beast," said Juanita Hensley, chief of driver services for the Division of Motor Vehicles, referring to the biblical significance of the number. "She said she did not want to be associated with the devil."

About 2,500 licenses were issued before officials decided to skip to 667, said Hensley, explaining, "I did not want 10,000 people calling me."

THE JERUSALEM SYNDROME CONTINUES

A Canadian tourist visiting Jerusalem became convinced that he was Samson and had to be sent to Kfar Shaul, Israel's Government Psychiatric Hospital. Once there he smashed through a wall to escape and was stopped at a bus stop by a nurse who said, "Samson, you must come back to the hospital." Doctors say the man complied because he was addressed by what he believed to be his true name. "He was our first Samson," said Dr. Yair Bar-El, director of the hospital. Every year dozens of tourists in Jerusalem inexplicably fall victim to the sickness; the deluded belief that they are indeed historical figures from biblical times. In another 1992 incident an American tourist ran amok at the Church of the Holy Sepulcher, breaking lamps, toppling a cross, and attempting to smash a Madonna statue, all the while screaming, "Suffer the little children. Do not worship idols."

THE "HELL FOUND" STORY

In case anyone had any doubts, the story about the Siberian research team digging down into the Earth and discovering Hell was a hoax. Rich Buhler, a Los Angeles radio host, reporting his findings in the July 1990 issue of *Christianity Today*, found the story published in a newsletter produced by Finnish missionaries who claimed it was originally published in a California paper. From there he traced it back to a Norwegian schoolteacher who circulated a "translation" of what was in fact a totally unrelated newspaper article written in Norwegian. The teacher then sent his original prank translation to a Texas evangelist, who apparently started the ball rolling toward worldwide dissemination of the story.

SPACED INVADER

As we reported last time, police were forced to shoot Rolf Rahn after a 16-hour standoff at his Genoa, New York, home when he pointed his gun at a police negotiator. Rahn had claimed to be an alien waiting for his spaceship to arrive. He shot a plumber who had come to his house because Rahn believed him to be an android. Rahn's dying words, "Feed my cats," led investigators to inspect his home several days later. There they found the freezer stuffed with 49 frozen cats of all ages and breeds and one rabbit. Each bag was tagged with the dates of death and freezing, the oldest dating to 1988. The labels also had information on which cats had been cooked in the oven to make them "pliable" for freezing. An animal control officer doubted that all 49 died from natural causes. An officer for the Society for Prevention of Cruelty to Animals was surprised to find a neat, clean kitchen. Two huge pans of clean litter were found in the pantry. The house had 15 rooms but Rahn apparently lived only in the kitchen.

THE BEES!

The Africanized honeybees, popularly feared as the killer bees, continued their march across Texas in 1992, moving through San Antonio, Corpus Christi, and Austin.

At Corpus Christi, they attacked a man mowing his lawn, stinging him 150 times. Juan J. Flores, 37, was rescued by neighbor Pete Cantu, who pulled him into his car. "The bees got into the car and they followed us," said Cantu. Flores recovered.

In Austin, Walter Theim, 71, and wife Elsie, 68, were attacked after spraying a hive with insecticide. Both were stung at least 20 times.

Dorothy Bird, a U.S. postmaster from Sebastian, Texas, was attacked by 400 bees in Santa Rosa, while running a weed eater. Her rescuers were also attacked.

Bee watchers said that by the summer of 1994, the killer bees will have swarmed into Arizona, California, Louisiana, and New Mexico.

NEW PLANET ISN'T

Noted British astronomer Andrew G. Lyne of the University of Manchester reported in July 1991 that he had detected a planet orbiting a neutron star 10,000 light years from Earth. Six months later, after further analyzing his data, he concluded that his calculations had been off and retracted the claim, explaining, "Our embarrassment is unbounded."

IS HE OR ISN'T HE?

Followers of Rabbi Menachem Mendel Schneerson, 90-year-old leader of the ultra-Orthodox Lubavitch Hasidic sect, still consider him to be the promised Messiah. In 1992, they rented billboards in Israel to proclaim "Prepare for the coming of the Messiah," amid belief that he would indeed go to Israel. In March he suffered a stroke that left him partly paralyzed and unable to speak. At one of his rare public appearances in early 1993, thousands gathered to plead with him to reveal himself as the Messiah. Schneerson appeared before the crowd for eight minutes, sitting in his wheelchair. His spokesperson said that the rabbi "is acknowledging nothing."

DIG IT

The New Age sect, Ministry of the Children, accepted responsibility for their September 1991 dig into the Bruton Parish churchyard in Williamsburg, Virginia. They had hoped to find a long-buried vault holding the writings of Sir Francis Bacon and a plan to save the world from destruction. In November, someone dug a 5½-foot to 7-foot-deep hole at the same location as the first dig. Finally, in August 1992 the church allowed a team of archaeologists to make the dig in hopes of once and for all putting an end to continued interest in the story. Weeks later the team found three 18th-century graves but no sign of the vault. Those supporting the vault theory said that the team looked in the wrong place and denounced the official dig as a cover-up.

BRONZE AGE DUDE

The "Iceman" found in the Austrian-Italian Alps continues to provoke debate over his age. Soon after our last volume went to press, a woman from Zurich came forward to say that she believed the mummified body to be that of her father, lost hiking in the region in the 1970s. She theorized he had tried to survive by fashioning primitive clothing and tools. Some archaeologists involved publicly admitted that a photo of the man did bear "a remarkable likeness" to the Iceman.

As to refining estimates of his age, University of Innsbruck researcher Klaus Oeggi said that his radio-carbon testing puts the find at 4,600 to 4,800 years old. Later, tests at Oxford showed the age to be about 5,300 years old.

SOURCES

The Anchorage Times
The Arizona Republic
Asahi Evening News (Tokyo)
The Asheville Citizen (North Carolina)
Associated Press
Atlanta Constitution
The Bangor Daily News (Maine)
The Beacon Journal (Cleveland)
The Bible Advocate
The Boston Globe
The Boston Herald
Brisbane Sunday Mail (Australia)
The Charlotte Observer
Chicago Sun-Times
Chicago Tribune

The Columbus Dispatch (Ohio)
Daily Mirror (U.K.)
Daily News (California)
Daily Telegraph (U.K.)
The Dallas Morning News
Denver Post
Des Moines Register
Details
Detroit Free Press
Detroit News
Deutsche Presse-Agentur
The Economist
Entertainment Weekly
The European
The Evening Sun (Baltimore)
Fortean Times
Fort Worth Star-Telegram
Glasgow Herald
The Globe and Mail
Harper's
Houston Post
The Independent (U.K.)
The International Herald Tribune
Johannesburg Star
The Journal (Knoxville)
The Journal (Milwaukee)
The Journal of Commerce
Kansas City Star
The Key West Citizen (Florida)
The Knoxville News-Sentinel (Tennessee)
The Lincoln Journal-Star (Nebraska)
London Times
Los Angeles Times
The Miami Herald

Minneapolis Star Tribune
The Morning Call (Allentown, Pennsylvania)
Nashville Banner (Tennessee)
New Haven Register
New Scientist
New York Daily News
New York Newsday
New York Post
The New York Times
Newsweek
The Olympian (Olympia, Washington)
Orange County Register (California)
The Oregonian
Parade
People
Philadelphia Daily News
The Philadelphia Inquirer
The Plain Dealer (Cleveland)
Pocono Record
The Post-Standard (Syracuse, New York)
The Press Democrat (Santa Rosa, California)
The Press-Sun Bulletin (Binghamton, New York)
The Raleigh News & Observer (North Carolina)
Record-Journal (Meriden, Connecticut)
Reuters
Rocky Mountain News
Roll Call
Saint Paul Pioneer Press
St. Louis Post-Dispatch
Saginaw News (Michigan)
The Salt Lake Tribune
San Francisco Chronicle
San Francisco Examiner
San Jose Mercury News (California)

The Scranton Times
Scripps-Howard
Seattle Post-Intelligencer
The Seattle Times
The Shreveport Times
Southeast Missourian (Cape Girardeau)
The Star-Ledger (Newark, New Jersey)
Strange Magazine
Sydney Morning Herald
Syracuse Herald-Journal (New York)
The Sun (Baltimore)
The Sunday Times (Scranton, Pennsylvania)
The Tampa Tribune
The Tennessean (Nashville)
Texas Monthly
Time
The Times-Leader (Wilkes-Barre, Pennsylvania)
The Times-Picayune (New Orleans)
Today London
The Toronto Sun (Ontario)
The Tribune (Scranton, Pennsylvania)
United Press International
USA Today
The Waco Tribune Herald (Texas)
The Wall Street Journal
The Washington Post
The Washington Times
Wellington Evening Post (New Zealand)

Plume

FROM MATRIMONY TO ALIMONY

☐ **A GROOM OF ONE'S OWN** *And Other Bridal Accessories* **by Mimi Pond.** How do you tie the knot and still keep your beau? Find out in this irreverent and indispensable guide for brides-to-be where you'll discover how your Perfect Wedding can go perfectly wrong and still be funny. (269458—$8.00)

☐ **WEDDING NIGHTMARES as told to the editors of** *Bride's* **magazine.** True tales of floral fiascos, ruinous receptions, honeymoon horrors, and other bridal calamities. Riotously funny stories of nuptials gone amok—offers a restorative dose of laughter for frayed nerves and short tempers. (267684—$7.00)

☐ **FROM "I DO" TO "I'LL SUE" by Jill Bauer.** This delightfully irreverent and amusing book is a must for anyone who's ever gone from matrimony to alimony. Filled with an entertaining array of quotes, fun facts, stranger-than-fiction true stories, and plenty of celebrated case histories, this witty survivors' guide takes you down the aisles and into the trials of some of the most famous and infamous divorces. (268591—$8.00)

Prices slightly higher in Canada.

Buy them at your local bookstore or use this convenient coupon for ordering.

PENGUIN USA
P.O. Box 999, Dept. #17109
Bergenfield, New Jersey 07621

Please send me the books I have checked above.
I am enclosing $_____ (please add $2.00 to cover postage and handling).
Send check or money order (no cash or C.O.D.'s) or charge by Mastercard or VISA (with a $15.00 minimum). Prices and numbers are subject to change without notice.

Card # _____ Exp. Date _____
Signature _____
Name _____
Address _____
City _____ State _____ Zip Code _____

For faster service when ordering by credit card call **1-800-253-6476**

Allow a minimum of 4-6 weeks for delivery. This offer is subject to change without notice